THE JEKYLL/HYDE SYNDROME

SYNDROME

Controlling Inner Conflict Through
Authentic Living

THE JEKYLL/HYDE SYNDROME

*Controlling Inner Conflict Through
Authentic Living*

by Mark McMinn

Barclay Press
Newberg, Oregon

THE JEKYLL/HYDE SYNDROME

Controlling Inner Conflict
Through Authentic Living

© 1996 Mark McMinn

International Standard Book Number 0-9-13342-79-3
Library of Congress Catalog Card Number: 96-083552

Cover by Donna Allison and Darren Gilroy
Interior design, composition, and lithography by Barclay Press,
Newberg, Oregon 97132, U.S.A.

Dedication

To Clark— a faithful friend.

THE JEKYLL/HYDE SYNDROME

Controlling Inner Conflict Through Authentic Living

A Word Before

What Keeps Me from Being Authentic?

Principles for Authentic Living

Conclusion: Practice Makes Better

Acknowledgments

Writing is a strange paradox. On the one hand, it is intensely personal—most of this book was constructed on my Macintosh computer in early morning hours of quiet and solitude. Yet on the other hand, writing is a product of social interactions. None of the ideas in this book belong to me. They are distilled from conversations and collaboration with friends, family, clients, students, and colleagues. To them I am grateful.

I was privileged to teach for nine years at George Fox College in Oregon. My faculty, staff, and administrative colleagues taught me to love liberal arts, to think carefully, and to value integrity. I am thankful for my many interactions with them—some on the basketball court, some in meetings or in the classroom, some at the lunch table.

As painful as it was to leave George Fox College, I have found my psychology associates at Wheaton College in Illinois to be equally supportive and helpful. My colleagues and students are idealists in the best sense—they motivate me by their vision, compassion, alertness, and incisive thinking.

Many of my clients have helped me understand human nature. Some of them overcame incredible odds to experience freedom from self-hatred and bitterness. And several close friends and family members have faced their pain publicly and honestly. I admire their stamina and have learned from their courage.

Lisa, my sociologist wife, has been directly involved in reading these words, suggesting changes, expanding my vision, and encouraging my ideas. And, more importantly, she faithfully endures the difficult seasons of marriage and celebrates the joyous ones—growing herself and helping me grow in authenticity.

As always, the staff at Barclay Press has been wonderful. Managing Editor Dan McCracken has encouraged me with his words and his example of quiet, faithful service to his calling. One of my best general psychology students ever, Jennifer Kinard, graduated as a writing/literature major and then started working for Barclay Press. She invested many hours in this manuscript, making excellent editorial changes. I have been privileged to publish with several large publishers throughout the country, but none have invested the time and care editing a manuscript that Barclay Press has, first with *Christians in the Crossfire* and now with this book.

There are three who have had no direct role in this book, but who inspire me by the way they live. My children, Danielle, Sarah, and Anna, amaze me with their flexibility, courage, and honesty. I hope and pray that the complexities of the world will never smother the God-given authenticity they have. Although I take seriously the position of authority I have over my children, sometimes I quietly think I want to be more like them when I grow up.

A Word Before

As a young enthusiastic college professor with three summer months ahead of me, I decided to write a book. Two hundred pages later, I felt I had written everything I knew—every proposition, every anecdote, every clinical example. Perhaps I had. It was a strange sensation, the draining of a mind. Yet, in another way, the writing had been exhilarating. Taking ideas, then organizing and communicating them, made them come alive to me. I started seeing myself and others differently. My teaching changed, my work as a psychologist changed, and my relationships changed. Undoubtedly I was the biggest benefactor of that first book. It wasn't bad and I was pleased to have it published as *Your Hidden Half* in 1988.

Shortly after it was published I realized why many of my bright colleagues had opted never to write books. People and ideas change but the printed word does not. Long after my summer at the word processor, people throughout the country were reading my words, even the words I later questioned. *Your Hidden Half* described the problem of conflicting human desires, but stopped short of practical strategies for change. After it was published and marketed, I wished I could change my conclusions and tell people there is more hope than I implied in the book. This is the plight of an author—to live with the discomfort of not being able to change one's words after a book is printed.

Happily, I've been given the chance to revise and add to the ideas in *Your Hidden Half*. Although some portions of this revision are similar to the original book, all of the chapters are new and many of the ideas have been improved because of life's persistent habit of pushing me toward maturity, even when I don't want to be pushed. I remain persuaded that private struggles haunt most of us from time to time and that our natural way of coping is to keep personal secrets and live with the shame secrecy produces. But there are better ways to manage our private struggles through developing a clear direction in life and authentic relationships with others.

Just as readers of the earlier version helped me refine my ideas, I welcome your comments and ideas on this book. Wisdom, I am finding, is a process more than a product and it only comes through authentic interactions with God, ideas, and others.

Mark McMinn
Wheaton, Illinois

PART I
WHAT KEEPS ME FROM BEING AUTHENTIC?

1

THE HONORABLE DR. JEKYLL
AND THE SECRET MR. HYDE

Those looking for a role model in nineteenth-century London would have idolized Dr. Henry Jekyll. He was bright, kind, gentle, wise, and wealthy. Some will argue that Dr. Jekyll wasn't real. He was, after all, the product of Robert Louis Stevenson's pen, a fictional character in *The Strange Case of Dr. Jekyll and Mr. Hyde*. But in another sense, Dr. Jekyll has always existed, timelessly reified in human nature. Perhaps it is our identification with Dr. Jekyll that makes Stevenson's story so convincing, so plausible.

If Dr. Jekyll were created today, he would still fit the archetype of perfection, but might look a bit different from the nineteenth-century Jekyll. Today, Jekyll would:

- Live in a 3,000-square-foot home with a 3-car garage,
- Coach his children's recreational teams,
- Encourage children to call him Henry,
- Have straight, white teeth,
- Be passionately concerned about homelessness and recycling,
- Have six months' salary in a savings account,
- Eat low-fat meals to keep himself fit and trim.

Does it all sound a bit unrealistic? Yes, but it may also sound strangely familiar. We identify with Dr. Jekyll because he lives inside each of us. We're busy showing others our best selves, and most of us are pretty good at it. So what do we see when we look around at

5

others we know? We see a lot of well-adjusted, sensitive, understanding, self-controlled, happy Dr. Jekylls.

As Stevenson's story unfolds, another side of Jekyll emerges. Jekyll concludes that "man is not truly one, but truly two." Hidden beneath layers of shame and secrecy, Jekyll was aware of his desires for pleasure and gratification. Jekyll wrote, "I was in no sense a hypocrite; both sides of me were in dead earnest." His dilemma is one we are all familiar with: how to allow pleasures in life while maintaining a reputation as an honorable person.

Jekyll, a brilliant chemist, developed a potion that allowed his evil side to emerge in the form of Mr. Edward Hyde, a small secretive man who lived out his impulses. At first he was delighted with his discovery because it was a perfect cover. "I was the first that could plod in the public eye with a load of genial respectability, and in a moment, like a schoolboy, strip off these lendings and spring headlong into the sea of liberty." But the story develops into a bitter battle between Jekyll and Hyde when Hyde begins appearing without invitation. Soon Hyde must take twice the normal potion to return to Jekyll. As the story reaches its tragic conclusion, Hyde has taken over completely and the only escape is suicide.

Mr. Hyde also sounds familiar to most of us. We look inside ourselves and see Mr. Hyde in our anger, temptation, despair, and evil. We sometimes conclude we are alone in our struggles, surrounded by Jekylls and fighting to maintain control over our desires and impulses. Ironically, we still put our "best foot forward" so when others look at us they only see Dr. Jekyll—the well-adjusted, self-controlled, understanding one. We compare the best in others with the worst in ourselves. In a culture addicted to approval, many people end up feeling phony, and no amount of social approval can make up for it.

Most of us know the feeling of having these two forces living in our bodies. Desires to be respected and admired fight desires for pleasure and gratification. The battle rages, riddling us as children, devastating us as adolescents, confusing us as adults, drawing its power from a seemingly endless reservoir. On one hand, we feel pressure to be honorable, even perfect, so we work to portray an image of responsibility, patience, and wisdom. On the other hand, our passions and desires for pleasure sometimes conflict with our public image.

We see this Jekyll/Hyde syndrome enacted all around us. Mr. A privately screams profanity at his children when they act irresponsibly, but treats them like royalty when they are in public. Pastor B's church releases him because of his extramarital affair with an active church member. Ms. C is swept away to a treatment facility for drug abuse, shocking those close to her who had no idea of her hidden addiction. Examples go on and on. It affects television evangelists, politicians, business executives, church leaders, homemakers, doctors, students, salespersons, and educators. Perhaps no one is completely exempt from the subtle pathology of the Jekyll/Hyde syndrome.

Showing Off Dr. Jekyll, Hiding Mr. Hyde

Most of us are quite good at identifying and modeling the upright Dr. Jekyll personality. We attend self-improvement seminars and listen to tapes to improve our self-esteem. We take off the "old self" and put on the "new self." We work all our lives to develop a solid reputation, to be kind and generous, gentle and understanding. And without even trying, we communicate that "good people" don't have unacceptable impulses and temptations.

Mr. Hyde is the hidden half and Dr. Jekyll is the visible half. Hyde isn't hidden to us personally—we all know we have an evil side. But we hide it in our social circles. It is more comfortable to talk about growth and progress and victories than about struggles and temptations. In our relentless quest for approval, we fear what others might think if we show our hidden selves.

We show off Dr. Jekyll—it is expected that we will. We protect ourselves by showing others what we want them to see—an outer layer that keeps others at a safe distance while impressing them with our apparent qualities. We keep Mr. Hyde safely buried inside, hoping he won't escape and cause public embarrassment.

Putting our best foot forward is nothing to be ashamed of. We do it naturally, perhaps out of biological instinct, in order to make ourselves attractive to others. And it usually works.

· ·

SELF-AWARENESS EXERCISE:

Try an experiment. Choose an upscale department store in your area and go shopping twice. The first time wear impressive clothing, the kind you might wear for a job interview. The second time wear very comfortable clothing, preferably something with some dirt or stains on it. Notice how other shoppers and store attendants react to you. Remember, they are not being intentionally rude. They are just reacting normally in a society that sees external appearance as paramount.

· ·

The Purpose of Dr. Jekyll

It seems right to criticize the Dr. Jekyll in each of us. Having an outer layer to impress others seems phony or hypocritical. I have sometimes referred to the Jekyll part of the personality as the **glossy side**, because it is designed to appear "slick" and be appealing to observers. Actually, the glossy side is an important part of human nature that plays an essential role in psychological adjustment.

From early infancy, it appears we are instinctively motivated to attach ourselves to others. At first, infants attach themselves to their caregivers by gazing into their eyes, crying when they leave the room, smiling when they return, and so on. These are instinctive behaviors that draw others close to the infant. As we grow, our attachment strategies change but the goal remains the same—to draw others close to us. Toddlers learn to share to maintain the approval of peers and parents. Schoolchildren quickly learn to follow rules to remain attached to their teachers. Adolescents wear the right jean labels and tennis shoes so their peers will accept them. Adults say the right things in public or drive stylish cars, sometimes for similar reasons.

The purpose of our Dr. Jekyll image is to draw others close to us. Those who are composed, beautiful, successful, and confident can do this most easily. Of course no one likes perfect people, so we often admit to minor mistakes to appear human. But even pointing out those mistakes can come from the glossy side, designed to impress others.

Thus, the glossy side is an essential tool for human attachment. Imagine a job interview without the capacity to impress the interviewer. Or picture meeting someone at a party without having the social graces necessary to carry on a conversation. Or imagine a schoolteacher trying to interest the pupils without having some flash in his or her personality. Dr. Jekyll plays an important role for each of us in our quest to attach to others.

The Purpose of Mr. Hyde

In Stevenson's novel, Jekyll went to extraordinary efforts to get rid of Hyde, just as we often do. So Jekyll didn't want Hyde, right? But wait a minute—Jekyll is the one who released Hyde, or what I sometimes call his **dark side**, in the first place. The quiet, well-mannered doctor wanted an alter ego to live out his fantasies. This is a classic example of ambivalence—loving and hating something or someone at the same time. Jekyll hated Hyde, and yet he loved Hyde. He wanted to get rid of Hyde, yet he wanted to keep and to nurture Hyde. Similarly, we like Mr. Hyde because we like pleasure, and we hate Mr. Hyde because we fear our drive for pleasure will get out of control.

Our drive for pleasure is an important part of human nature. Can you imagine what life would be like without it? Perhaps we would work 16 hours a day, eat lots of vegetables, avoid friendships and romance, and clean house and watch documentaries in our spare time.

Take human sexuality as an example. Sexual urges and fantasies cause all kinds of problems in our culture. But think for a moment about life without sexual pleasure. Marriages, if they existed at all, would lose much of their intimacy. Dating and courting would become mundane tasks of adolescence and early adulthood, like choosing an apartment or a college to attend. We would have to develop social incentives to increase birth rates throughout the world. Advertising executives for car and beer companies would be out of work. Life would lose some of its joy.

Just as Dr. Jekyll plays an important role in the human personality, so does Mr. Hyde. The goal of authentic living is not to rid ourselves of Jekyll or Hyde, but to move beyond them.

Beyond Jekyll and Hyde

Many relationships flourish by remaining on the surface—the business associates who enjoy golfing together, the Wednesday morning bridge group, the neighborhood softball team. But the deepest, most intimate relationships move beyond superficiality and require the risk of truly revealing ourselves to another.

Consider two questions:

- How did I feel last time I confided one of my "secrets" to a trustworthy friend?
- How did that friend help me understand myself better?

For most of us, these questions demonstrate the importance of authenticity—being our whole selves around those we trust the most. Of course you may also recall times when you tried to be unrealistically authentic. Perhaps you shared too much with a casual acquaintance and later found your transparency was fuel for the gossip mill. Or maybe even the trustworthy friend hasn't always been trustworthy or your friend's well-intentioned responses only made matters worse. These bad experiences sometimes keep us in our protective shell, hesitating to take risks and be real with those around us. Sometimes we don't even admit the truth to ourselves because the risk of knowing feels too great.

Although the Jekyll image plays an important role in relating to others, and the Hyde image allows us to experience pleasure, moving toward greater authenticity requires moving beyond Jekyll and Hyde in two ways. First, we need to develop deep self-understanding. It is not enough to know our strengths and weaknesses, the ways others perceive us, and our style of relating to them. We need to know ourselves deeply—our passions, values, and dreams, our struggles and temptations. Second, to move toward authenticity we need to usher others into our inner life, allowing them to love us as we are, not as we wish to appear. We need to move beyond Dr. Jekyll and Mr. Hyde in our perceptions of ourselves and in our intimate relationships.

Take a look at the bookstore shelves sometime—they're a good barometer of our culture. Some shelves are piled high with books about pleasure—how to enjoy better sex, find happiness in your career, fulfill your potential, make more money, plan for retirement, and protect your rights. Most of them could have been written by Mr. Hyde. Other shelves are piled high with books on dressing for success, thinking positively, influencing people, and designing polished presentations. Most of them could have been written by Dr. Jekyll. But feeling sexy, honorable, successful, or wealthy is not enough. We need to authentically know ourselves and others, and allow others to know us before we can experience personal wholeness.

2

LOOKING OUT FOR NUMBER ONE

Often the pleasures of life become the greatest tragedies. I see it regularly as a psychotherapist. The innocent trip to Las Vegas ends up canceling years of savings. Flirting at the office turns into split families and abandoned children. The drink to relax after work leads to a struggle with addiction, lost relationships and self-respect, and financial ruin.

The same was true for Dr. Jekyll. It started as the perfect scheme—relegate the evil to its own person so Jekyll could escape the criticism and embarrassment of seeking personal pleasures. And Mr. Hyde knew pleasure. As the potion created Mr. Hyde for the first time, Jekyll wrote:

> There was something strange in my sensations, something indescribably new and, from its very novelty, incredibly sweet. I felt younger, lighter, happier in body; within I was conscious of a heady recklessness, a current of disordered sensual images running like a millrace in my fancy, a solution of the bonds of obligation, an unknown but not an innocent freedom of the soul. I knew myself, at the first breath of this new life, to be more wicked, tenfold more wicked, sold a slave to my original evil; and the thought, in that moment braced and delighted me like wine.

But his scheme turned sour as Mr. Hyde began to usurp more and more control. After Hyde abused a child and murdered a man, he was forced into hiding and Jekyll worked with all his might to keep Hyde from reappearing. But Hyde kept coming back, even without the potion. The final tragic solution came with the words that close Stevenson's book: "Here then, as I lay down the pen and proceed to seal up my confession, I bring the life of that unhappy Henry Jekyll to an end."

One possible interpretation is that we should avoid pleasures since pleasures sometimes lead to ruin. We blame the demise on Mr. Hyde and believe everything would have been okay if Dr. Jekyll remained in control. We see Jekyll as the good guy and Hyde as the bad guy— opposites in the struggle for morality. But were they really opposites?

It is true that Jekyll and Hyde had different goals. Jekyll wanted to appear perfect. He represented the outer layer, the persona that is portrayed to others. Hyde wanted to experience pleasure, even pleasure that was socially disgraceful. But despite their disparate goals, several commonalties suggest they were not opposites.

First, both Jekyll and Hyde were stubbornly independent. Hyde came and went as he wished, entering Jekyll's house through the back alley door. He took orders from no one, not even Jekyll. In fact, he joyfully defied the orders and expectations of others. Jekyll also was stubbornly independent. After he discovered his problem keeping Hyde suppressed, he isolated himself in his house, accepting no visitors and seeking help from no one.

Stubborn independence hinders authenticity, whether it comes from our outer layer (Jekyll) or our inner passions (Hyde). For example, imagine a friend of yours, Frank, invites you to his house for dinner. You are immediately impressed with the furnishings of his home. Original oil paintings adorn the walls, antique furniture enhances the beautiful hardwood floors. Dinner is served on expensive china accented with silver and crystal. Throughout dinner Frank discusses his upcoming vacation to the Bahamas. You are impressed. What you don't know is that Frank doesn't earn enough for his lifestyle. He has two mortgages on his home, five credit cards run to their limit, and debts to pay on numerous household furnishings.

Frank is stubbornly independent about his problem. While his possessions may add to his social appeal (at least he thinks so), he does not consult with others before adding more possessions. To do so would risk others finding out about his spending problem. Neither does he confide in others about his compulsive spending problems, because he fears disapproval. He remains stubbornly independent, both in the outer layer, which accumulates material possessions and in the inner passions, which lead to reckless spending.

Second, both Jekyll and Hyde were impulsive. They acted before carefully considering the consequences. Jekyll acted impulsively to maintain his reputation, Hyde to pursue sensual pleasures. In the end, both committed a heinous, impulsive act: murder. Hyde murdered another and Jekyll murdered himself.

Making decisions without considering the consequences often hinders authenticity. Consider Mike, a happily married business executive. He enjoys evening chats with his wife, Saturday bike rides with his children, and considers himself a faithful family man. But lately he has been catching prolonged glances from his wife's friend, Janice. He has started noticing her pleasant smile and attractive way of dressing. Sometimes Mike is preoccupied with Janice while sitting at his desk attempting to complete paperwork. Occasionally he drives by Janice's house on his way home from work and hopes she is working in the front yard or arriving home at the same time. His job performance is suffering, he is more irritable with his children, and his wife has commented that he seems distant. He enjoys the feelings of attraction, but is tired of struggling to maintain an upright appearance. How can he cope?

Hyde wants pleasure. Jekyll wants a flawless image. But both are impulsive. One part (Hyde) will tell Mike to pursue Janice, no matter what the cost. The other will tell him to keep his struggles private, no matter what the cost. But impulsive actions will only bring grief.

Once Mike concludes that his conflict has no immediate solution, he might begin to look more closely at his experience rather than desperately scrambling for recipe-like answers. He might ask what he can learn about himself from this attraction. He might take the risk of discussing his dilemma with a close, trustworthy friend. In exploring his feelings and investigating his motives he might better understand his priorities and values, the meaning of marital fidelity, the devastating consequences of infidelity, and the importance of moral standards. He might learn more about grace and love and pain. He will grow only as he moves away from the impulsiveness of the Jekyll/Hyde syndrome.

Third, Jekyll and Hyde were both rigid and inflexible. Neither was willing to compromise his extreme position. Jekyll was committed to the persona of perfection and Hyde to the pursuit of pleasure. Both reacted defensively when challenged.

John was a successful physician who finally agreed to marital therapy when Susan threatened to leave him. His many friends considered him a pillar of his community, and he was well-respected by his colleagues. "This is not my fault," he insisted, as he pointed the blame toward Susan. But Susan lived under the cloud of his rigidity and inflexibility. His schedule was nonnegotiable. He came and went as he pleased, worked 70 hour weeks, spent large sums of money without consulting her, ignored the children, and became angry if she disapproved. Over time, the reason for his rigidity became clear—he was protecting himself from others because of the secrets he was working to maintain. He managed to keep his extramarital affair a secret from Susan for a year and from his therapist for six months. He kept his tax fraud a secret from everyone until the IRS caught him. John was caught in the Jekyll/Hyde syndrome.

As we have seen, Jekyll and Hyde are not opposites. They are similar: both stubbornly independent, impulsive, rigid, and inflexible. In sum, both Jekyll and Hyde are **self-focused**. They both look to protect their own interests: public approval for Jekyll and personal pleasure for Hyde. Self-focus is an obstacle to authenticity.

Beyond Jekyll and Hyde

Fortunately, Stevenson doesn't capture the entire human personality in his story of Dr. Jekyll and Mr. Hyde. We have more noble qualities than those reflected in the approval-seeking Jekyll and the pleasure-seeking Hyde.

••

SELF-AWARENESS EXERCISE:

Think of the last time you were helpful to someone else. Also think of the last book you found fascinating. And think of a time when you changed your mind when discussing an idea with someone. Now for each of these situations, ask yourself if you were acting more like the approval-seeking Jekyll or the pleasure-seeking Hyde. Spend some time doing this before reading ahead.

Did you find it difficult to decide whether you were thinking and acting as Jekyll or Hyde? If so, it is because these behaviors—helping others, pursuing knowledge, and being convinced of another opinion—are usually not self-focused. Instead, these behaviors point to a more noble part of the human character.

• •

In addition to our self-focused facets, humans have the ability to be **truth-focused**, to use creativity and intellect to see beyond ourselves and our personal desires; to transcend self-focus and see a bigger picture.

Psychologist Erich Fromm labeled humans the "freaks" of the universe because, unlike the rest of the animal kingdom, we have both animal impulses and reasoning capabilities. The animal impulses cause us to desire food, sex, pleasure, avoidance of pain, and so forth. They also cause us to seek approval and form attachments with others. But with every impulse, we also have the ability to reason, giving us the capacity for self-control and good judgment.

Much of our humanity is comprised of our ability to be truth-centered. This truth-focused part of our nature allows us to be interdependent, insightful, and adaptable.

Interdependent. Whereas Jekyll and Hyde were stubbornly independent, our truth-centered facet allows us to cooperate with others by helping them and allowing them to help us. This facet allows us to accept others without being threatened by their strengths or feeling superior because of their weaknesses. Those searching for truth feel genuine concern for the big problems in life. They care about social issues such as hunger, violence, and prejudice. They establish meaningful, authentic relationships with close friends.

Psychologist Abraham Maslow conducted an extensive study[1] of those who had moved beyond self-focus to pursue truth (he called them self-actualizers, not to be confused with selfish). He then described some of their common characteristics, including:

- Fellowship with humanity. They identify with others and with the human condition.

[1]A. H. Maslow, *Motivation and Personality* 2nd ed. (New York: Harper & Row 1970)

- Profound interpersonal relationships. They form deep, loving bonds with others.
- Acceptance of self and others. They are able to accept the short-comings of themselves and others, recognizing that no one can become perfect.

Notice how these characteristics suggest interdependence, an authentic, caring connection between people.

When we are truth-focused, we are not greatly moved either by flattery or criticism. We are more concerned with issues of truth and justice than self-image and reputation. Those who are interdependent are able to love the essence of another person, regardless of worldly status or possessions. This is the love the Good Samaritan showed to the penniless victim dying on the side of the road. In contrast, self-focus leads to a narcissistic love motivated by meeting one's own needs.

Insightful. Jekyll and Hyde were impulsive, acting on self-interest without considering the bigger picture. Although the truth-focused inner life leaves plenty of room for spontaneity, people and events are seen in a larger context and decisions are made after considering the welfare of others. Insight allows us to see beyond ourselves, listen keenly to others, and center our lives around important values and priorities. Several of Maslow's characteristics of self-actualizers point to insight.

- Task-centered. They see some mission in life beyond meeting their own needs.
- Accurate perception of reality. They are able to discern what is honest and true from what is dishonest and false.
- Peak experiences. They have frequent experiences of sensing deep meaning and harmony with nature or others.
- Continued freshness of appreciation. They appreciate nature and often feel awed by everyday displays of beauty, such as a flower or a sunset.

Insightful individuals usually function in conventional ways, but are not bound to conventional behaviors. They break the mold when necessary. They have a clear sense of morality, but do not have to conform to please others. The Jewish religious leaders were angered when Jesus broke the custom by healing a man's hand on the Sabbath. But his behavior was both spontaneous and moral. The leaders objected because of their self-righteous impulsive conformity to the Old Testament law.

Insightful individuals lack phoniness. They are comfortable accepting themselves and are willing to show their true selves to others. One person does a good act to be noticed, another does the same act out of genuine compassion. There is a difference. One comes from self-focus, the other from truth-focus.

Adaptable. Jekyll and Hyde are rigid and inflexible, but the inner truth-focused life allows us to adapt to a variety of situations, coping with the stresses and appreciating the joys of each. Maslow's characteristics of self-actualizers hint at this ability to adapt.

- Spontaneity. They are spontaneous, creative, and enthusiastic.
- Autonomy. They are resourceful, good problem-solvers, and enjoy working alone when necessary.
- Unhostile sense of humor. They can laugh at themselves and human shortcomings.

One biblical writer wrote from a prison cell that he had learned to be content in any situation. That kind of adaptability cannot be found in the approval-seeking of Dr. Jekyll or the pleasure seeking of Dr. Hyde. It can only be found by looking for meaning, and finding a sense of purpose and truth beyond ourselves.

| CHARACTERISTICS OF SELF-FOCUS AND TRUTH-FOCUS ||
Self-focus	*Truth-focus*
Stubborn independence	Interdependence
Impulsive	Insightful
Rigid and inflexible	Adaptable

Jekyll keeps us trying to look good, covering up our flaws. Hyde keeps us seeking personal pleasure. Both move us away from accurate self-understanding and authentic encounters with others. Our truth-focused nature brings acceptance of others, spontaneity, social awareness, genuine loving, and authenticity. To become authentic people, we must move beyond self-focus in search of truth.

3

TUG OF WAR

When Colonel James Irwin, former astronaut and one of the few persons to walk on the moon, came to speak at the local college, we took our three daughters to hear him. He gave an outstanding talk that was as interesting to my grade school daughters as it was to the college students, faculty, and staff. The next morning we were reflecting on Colonel Irwin's talk around the breakfast table. Our oldest daughter, who was amazed at how much fuel it required to get a rocket out of the atmosphere, asked how the rocket gets down once it reenters the earth's atmosphere. I answered, *"Gravity* pulls you down." Sarah, then six years old, looked troubled and immediately blurted, "Gravity? Who is he?"

In one sense, Sarah knew a lot about gravity. She knew not to jump from high places and she enjoyed dropping paper scraps from our loft balcony, pretending they were snow flakes falling to the ground. But in another sense she wasn't familiar with the concept of gravity.

I believe in emotional gravity. Just as physical gravity pulls us back to our home planet, emotional gravity pulls us back to the tendencies we try hardest to outgrow. When faced with stress or temptation, our natural inclination is to return to old coping patterns. When moving toward authenticity, it is natural to make progress and then slip back to our self-focused inclinations when times get rough. A significant obstacle to authenticity is the gravitational pull of Jekyll and Hyde in dragging us back to self-centered ways of thinking and relating to others.

The Good and the Bad

Generally, we work to remove bad and add good in our lives. Smokers try to quit their habit because it leads to health problems. We labor through jogging or stationary bicycling because exercise is good. The difficult choices come when something is a mixture of good and bad. Going to the dentist is a difficult choice for some because they want their teeth fixed (good), but they don't want the pain of the dental procedure (bad). Jekyll and Hyde would be easier to resist if they weren't a mixture of good and bad.

The Jekyll side of personality is good, as mentioned earlier, because it appeals to others. It helps us meet attachment needs. It is bad when it dominates the way we relate to others. Intimate friendships are never built by knowing only the surface of another. The Hyde side of personality is also good because it keeps us looking for variety and pleasure in life. But when it dominates it becomes bad because the search for pleasure gets out of control. Allocating too much power to either Jekyll or Hyde is an obstacle to authenticity.

Hyde's Pull

Stevenson wrote of Hyde, "His every act and thought centered on self." What is attractive about Mr. Hyde, and why is it difficult to escape the gravitational pull of Hyde's self-focus? There are several responses to these questions, all related to our ways of thinking about a situation.

It can be secret. So far we have discussed Mr. Hyde as a personality force that seeks pleasure, but part of seeking pleasure is avoiding pain, including the pain of others knowing our secrets. Mr. Hyde seduces us by telling us whatever we do will remain a secret forever.

As a psychologist, I am persuaded that keeping secrets leads to many emotional problems. Many times clients have expressed relief after unveiling a long-standing secret. Secrets erode the human spirit and cause more damage with each passing year. Although I'm not sure why secrets have this effect, I suspect it may be because we are created to be social beings and therefore have an instinctual longing to reveal ourselves to others. When we deny those instincts by keeping secrets, feelings of sadness, loneliness, and depression warn us that something is wrong.

Authenticity requires us to cautiously unload our secrets. Mike goes to coffee with his longtime (and trustworthy) friend, Bill, who asks, "How are things going for you, Mike?" Mike says:

A. "Things are going fine, Bill. I sold more this month at work than I have for three years. Things are really great."
B. "My wife is just so hard to get along with. I'm considering leaving her."
C. "I've got a problem that I need to talk with someone about. Do you have some time to listen?"

Only one of these responses will build authenticity. Response A simply denies any problem. Many friendships function well at this level, but Mike and Bill are intimate, trusting friends and Mike is denying the truth with response A. Response B is more open, but Mike is not being honest with himself by blaming his wife for his feelings. Response C opens the door for honest communication where Mike can tell Bill his inner feelings and struggles. Only with response C will Mike be understanding and revealing his deepest feelings—feelings he has kept to himself for many weeks.

Maybe secrets are hard to discuss because they force us to admit the selfish parts of our nature. But as we take the risk and open up to our closest friends, they are also more inclined to relate authentically in return.

It will be fun. Another appeal of Mr. Hyde is our natural desire for immediate pleasure. It's hard to say no when saying yes is more fun.

I remember my first cake-baking experience. I had never baked a birthday cake for Lisa, my wife, before. She was gone for a couple hours so I went to the store and picked up a cake mix and a box of frosting. Feeling quite domestic, I sat the children on the kitchen counter, pulled the round, perfect-looking cake from the oven and began mixing the frosting. I was hungry.

Using my creative genius, I invented an idea for a different style of birthday cake—a square one. Simply by cutting off the edges of the round cake, I could make a square one. Of course the real motivation (and the real genius) was that I could then eat the cut-off pieces. The cake was truly delicious though the square cake was smaller than I had anticipated.

If I had ever frosted a cake before I would have realized my folly. I would have known that frosting does not stick to a crumbly, cut surface. But instead I tried for many frustrating minutes to put frosting over my now square cake. The cake got smaller and smaller and the frosting became more and more lumpy with crumbs. It eventually looked like a casserole from a seventh grade home economics class. The reality of my failure fell upon me suddenly as my four-year-old daughter looked thoughtfully at the mess and then cautiously asked, "Dad, how many cakes have you made before?" I gave up on my square cake. On my second trip to the store, the clerk assured me that no one could foul up making a cake with a mix. I assured her that I could.

Only part of the problem was culinary inexperience. The bigger problem was that I did not delay gratification. I could have waited two hours for dinner, but I wanted the taste of that cake right then. The self-focused part of my personality triumphed by insisting that I needn't wait for gratification. I could have my cake and eat it too.

It's someone else's problem. Another appealing aspect of Mr. Hyde is the casual attitude we can take toward responsibility. Just as it's hard to say no when saying yes is more fun, it's hard to say yes when saying no can allow life to be easier.

Our society has focused on personal rights and assertiveness to the point where we often ignore community responsibilities. In the Bible, after Cain murdered his brother Abel, God asked Cain, "Where is your brother?" Cain's response, "Am I my brother's [or sister's] keeper?" is the heresy of our society. The implied answer in the biblical account, as it ought to be in contemporary society, is yes, to some extent we are responsible to care for one another.

Let's imagine you arrive home from the variety store after purchasing a number of household items, look at the receipt, and realize you were not charged for a $72 barbecue. Mr. Hyde would recommend keeping quiet, enjoying the barbecue, and finding another way to spend the $72. Avoiding responsibility is pleasurable, and easily justified: "It's their mistake. Why should I bother with it?" But the truth-focused part of your personality might give a more holistic response as you think about the plight of the store clerk, the manager, and other consumers who pay higher prices because of similar losses. You conclude you are your brothers' and sisters' keeper as you pick up the telephone.

It's only natural. Mr. Hyde can also seduce us by pointing out biological urges: "It's only natural you act this way, so don't hold back." The dark side comes from our biological nature, from animal urges like aggression and sex.

The human capacity for aggression is mind-boggling. In the name of defense and peace, we now have the ability to destroy the world over two dozen times. Fifty-five million people were killed during World War II alone, with Hitler killing up to six thousand Jews per day. Plotless films filled with automatic weapons and needless destruction fill theaters and break box office records.

These urges also affect domestic life. The typical mother speaks irritably to her children once every two to three minutes. Often parental aggression takes more extreme forms of yelling, harsh discipline, or unnecessary restriction.

Anger and aggressive urges appear to be wired into our brains at birth. The limbic system is a series of circuits deep inside the human brain that cause humans and animals to express anger and rage. Is Hyde right that aggression can't be helped because it is natural? Fortunately not. The human brain also has a highly developed cortex, an outer layer that allows us to pursue more than self-interest. The cortex enables us to think critically, control impulses, and exercise good judgment. So humans will experience anger and feel aggressive, but they have the capacity to make choices contrary to what might seem natural, even in the midst of angry feelings.

Sexuality is another natural facet of the human experience, but Mr. Hyde would have us use nature to justify irresponsible sexual expressions. And sexual conflicts are widespread. Numerous studies have investigated sexual behavior and found some dismal statistics. Unfaithfulness, promiscuity, and sexual addictions, though often kept secret, haunt millions in our society.

Even in the aftermath of our overt sexual revolution and in what some would consider a sexually addicted culture, we lack healthy discussions of our sexuality. One cartoon shows a grade school boy whispering to another, "I finally found out what sex is; my sister plays one in the school band." Because of our reticence to discuss sex, we don't share our sexual conflicts with others. We relegate the sexual conflicts to the secret Mr. Hyde so nobody can see them.

Authentic living requires us to deal boldly with our natural urges—not to deny them, but to handle them responsibly. Through self-understanding and close, confiding relationships with others those impulses that rule animal behavior can be altered by humankind's unique ability to be truth-focused as well as self-focused.

••

SELF-AWARENESS EXERCISE:

List three pleasurable things you have done today. They can be simple things—watching a show on television, receiving a back rub, eating dessert, and so on. For each of the three things you listed, write about how that activity could be a problem if it were taken to an extreme. For example, the pleasure of watching television could be a problem if you watched ten hours of television a day. Receiving a back rub could be a problem if you felt a need to be touched in similar ways by numerous casual acquaintances. Eating dessert may be a problem if you eat four or five helpings.

If any of these three pleasures were to carry you to the extreme you just wrote about, which of the following would you be likely to use to justify your desire for pleasure?

A. It can be secret.
B. It will be fun.
C. It's someone else's problem.
D. It's only natural.

This exercise shows our human attraction toward Mr. Hyde. Our drive for pleasure is healthy in moderate doses, but can be destructive in heavy doses.

••

Jekyll's Pull

The Dr. Jekyll side of personality has its own attraction, resulting in a gravitational pull toward approval-seeking.

Covering our messes. Jekyll appeals to us by telling us to cover the messes that Hyde creates. In Stevenson's story, Dr. Jekyll became more and more consumed with covering up for Hyde's indiscretions. By the end, Jekyll is spending all day every day covering for Hyde.

The political scandals of recent decades have had more to do with cover-ups than with initial offenses. The Watergate scandal of the Nixon administration would have been received more kindly if it weren't for the cover-up. The congressional bank scandal and the post office scandal would have been second or third page news if it weren't for efforts to cover up. If a male senator coerces a woman for sexual favors, it is a terrible offense. But if the same senator then threatens and intimidates the woman so she won't report the offense, he has magnified the evil tenfold.

Cover-ups are tempting because they work sometimes. Picture Nita, a woman with a compulsive spending problem, as she enters the house after an afternoon at the mall. "Did you buy anything?" her husband, Rob, asks nervously.

"No, just did some window shopping," Nita replies, hoping he won't look in the trunk before she has a chance to smuggle her new clothes into the bedroom. Two days later, the new clothes lie safely in the dresser and Nita's cover-up has worked beautifully. Jekyll has covered for Hyde, and Nita has avoided Rob's criticism. "Besides," she reasons, "it would only hurt Rob to know the truth." The problem is that Nita continues to live inauthentically, and her approval-seeking behavior is self-focused rather than truth-focused.

The honor of wisdom. Another pull toward approval-seeking is the supposed wisdom of Jekyll. Our glossy side desires to appear wise and honorable to others. One way we do that is by giving advice and answers to those with questions.

I tell my counseling students there are two rules about giving advice. First, never give advice. Second, give advice sometimes. But they have to learn the first rule before they can learn the second. Sometimes answers are useful, but the person who always has an answer is probably responding more from his or her own need than from genuine concern for others.

For example, Alice confides to her friend Shelly that life has been a struggle lately. Alice feels blue, thinks poorly of herself, and sees very little hope in the future. Shelly listens politely and then says that God causes these things to work together for good and that prayer and Bible study will help Alice regain enthusiasm for life. Alice leaves feeling misunderstood, guilty, and unspiritual.

Shelly's answer did not address the depth of depression Alice experienced. It was a recipe answer, lacking a true understanding of the problem. If we could get inside Shelly's head, we might have observed thoughts such as:

> Alice is trusting me with this information. I have to have something good to say. If I don't come up with a good answer, she'll think I'm not listening or that I don't care.

Notice that Shelly is not trying to hurt Alice. In fact, she has some genuine concern. But her greatest concern is looking good in front of Alice and perhaps impressing Alice with her wisdom. Shelly's glossy side is propelling her answer.

The competitive urge. The need to have an answer is probably related to self-esteem. If I have an answer for every question of yours, then I know more than you. That makes me wise and honorable. Dr. Jekyll shines.

This suggests another way Dr. Jekyll pulls us in. We sometimes criticize or judge others because of our competitive nature and our desire to be better than others. Just as having an answer for every problem builds self-esteem; so does pointing out faults in others. What if Shelly told Alice that her depression was the result of sin in her life? This kind of counsel is not uncommon.

Even among those of us who see ourselves as accepting and non-judgmental, the glossy side is more powerful than we often think. I realized this when I found myself on the unfamiliar side of a psychologist's desk. Though I had always told my clients that seeking counseling was not a sign of personal weakness, deep inside I felt a judgmental sense of moral superiority. When I needed a psychologist, I had to confront my judgmental attitude and my neurotic belief that I should always be giving help rather than receiving help.

Coping with life's problems is a complicated process and many problems defy easy answers. Judging others for their emotional problems only causes them to mask their unhealthy desires, increasing their reliance on Dr. Jekyll.

"Should" versus "why." Another reason we sometimes rely too much on our glossy side is because it allows us to function with very little thinking. This outer rim of our personality is concerned most about seeking approval, and often includes a set of socially accepted views or recipes for successful living. Those dominated by the glossy side don't have to think about tough issues because they already have their mind made up.

This probably starts when, as children, we learn to get approval by obeying without thinking. "Dad, why do I have to pick up the toys in my bedroom?" "Because I said so — just do it!" It is easy to establish arbitrary authority with children and to quell that natural desire they have to know why. As a result, parents sometimes teach children that "shoulds" have no "whys."

But as adults we still sometimes believe in "shoulds" without "whys." We try living by the recipes we learned earlier in life and feel surprised when things don't work out predictably. Lawrence Kohlberg and other moral development researchers argue that the majority of adults make moral decisions based upon the letter of the law. Most define right and wrong with "shoulds" and not with "whys."

The religious leaders of Jesus' day followed the letter of the law. They insisted the disciples of Jesus refrain from picking a few handfuls of wheat on the Sabbath. They were just reflexively responding to the outer layer of morality they had been taught, and not looking for reasons behind their "shoulds" and "should nots." Jesus reminded the Pharisees of the Old Testament account of David eating the sacred bread when he needed food while running from Israel's King Saul. Jesus made his point well. "Shoulds" are shallow unless backed up with "whys."

The "shoulds" of the glossy side may simplify life's decisions, but they lead us away from an authentic encounter with truth and encourage self-focus. Every time we violate a "should," we feel guilty and become more self-focused. The thoughts might go like this:

> "No one else I know feels like they are tired of their kids."
> "If I were healthy and well-adjusted, I wouldn't be noticing attractive co-workers at the office."
> "If others knew about this temptation, I would be asked to resign from the deacon board."

And so on. These thoughts are not based on truth, but on approval-seeking and "shoulds"—"I shouldn't have this problem."

Let me quickly add that I am not opposed to "shoulds." Most of the rules of life are designed to keep us out of trouble, and it would be foolish to recklessly challenge every rule. We don't need to give up the "shoulds," we just need to understand the "whys."

•••

SELF-AWARENESS EXERCISE:

Try applying the principles of this chapter while listening to a call-in radio talk show. Listen to both the callers and the hosts and try to identify the voice of Jekyll. Listen for those giving easy answers, "shoulds," or judging others harshly. Can you hear a difference between those honestly looking to find truth and those trying to impress others?

Jekyll and Hyde each have their own attraction, their own gravitational pull, making decisions more complicated. But the more energy we spend on the pleasure-seeking Hyde or the approval-seeking Jekyll, the more self-absorbed we become and the less we seek truth. Authenticity requires fighting the subtle pull of Jekyll and Hyde.

•••

4

THE BATTLE OF JEKYLL AND HYDE

In the film *The Empire Strikes Back* the great Jedi master, Yoda, was training young Luke Skywalker to become a Jedi knight. Luke feared that the evil side of "The Force" would become too strong if not destroyed immediately. He sensed evil in a nearby cave and approached the cave with caution. Yoda called out, "Your weapons, you will need them not." Luke ignored Yoda and entered the cave with his laser sword at his side. Suddenly the evil Darth Vader seemed to appear in the cave. The sword fight was brief as Luke lopped off Vader's head. But as the black helmet lay on the ground, Skywalker's own face gradually appeared beneath the face shield. Had Luke killed part of himself?

The potential for evil is as dissonant for us as it was for Skywalker. We want to destroy evil and live in peace. We want to remove temptation and live in clarity. So we take up our swords impulsively to purge evil by destroying it. Yet, in the name of purging evil, we end up attacking part of ourselves. Killing Mr. Hyde is not the answer.

What did Yoda have in mind when he told Skywalker not to take his weapon? Perhaps Yoda knew that the evil Luke was about to confront was his own. It could not be destroyed with weapons; it could only be understood.

So it is with us. In fear that our dark side will take over, we seek to destroy it. We swing our weapons wildly. We use the arbitrary "shoulds," the easy answers, and the judgmental perspectives of the glossy side. We strike down our dark side and feel immediate relief.

But gradually we become aware that we have futilely attempted to eradicate a part of ourselves. Mr. Hyde returns more determined than ever.

Hyde Won't Die

What do we lose by trying to kill our dark sides? We lose authenticity. David is a pastor and well-respected by his parishioners. He speaks frequently about the evils of movies and television, and refrains from card-playing, dancing, and drinking. Last week he delivered a persuasive sermon entitled "Forsaking All Others," arguing that faithfulness to one's spouse starts by not having friends of the opposite sex. People see David as pious and committed to his faith. But underneath the controlled outer layer of his life, David struggles with a life of chaos. Every month or so, David drives an hour out of town to an adult bookstore, buys a pornographic magazine, and masturbates in his car. He feels shame each time, and vows to keep himself pure by avoiding women more. But all his efforts to kill his dark side don't work and a month later he's back in the adult bookstore.

David is caught in a trap, trying to kill part of himself that can never be killed. He ends up living part of his life in secret, caught in a cycle of inauthenticity. Let's take a close look at the trap David is in.

JEKYLL TRYING TO ELIMINATE HYDE

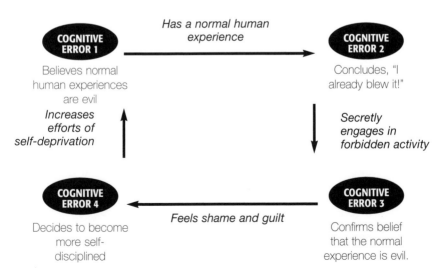

David is engaging in what psychologists call "cognitive errors," faulty ways of thinking that affect his feelings and behavior. There are four cognitive errors in this example, one in each corner of this diagram. First, David incorrectly assumes a normal human behavior is evil. He and his counselor try to reconstruct what happened before he left town for the adult bookstore.

> COUNSELOR: Tell me what was going on just before you decided to go to the bookstore.
>
> DAVID: I had just been counseling with a member of my congregation.
>
> COUNSELOR: What can you tell me about the counseling session?
>
> DAVID: Well, my client is having a tough time in her marriage. I remember feeling bad after the session was over.
>
> COUNSELOR: Let's imagine there was a tape recorder capturing your thoughts as that session ended. We're going to replay it now. What is on the tape?
>
> DAVID: Guilt.
>
> COUNSELOR: Guilt?
>
> DAVID: Yeah, I remember feeling guilty because of my thoughts about her.
>
> COUNSELOR: Tell me about your thoughts.
>
> DAVID: Well, I guess I find her attractive.
>
> COUNSELOR: So you were feeling guilty because you found her attractive.
>
> DAVID: Yes. I'm happily married. I don't know what's wrong with me.

David's assumption is that finding a woman attractive is an evil act of betrayal for a married man. So he feels guilty. The first cognitive error is complete.

We all find other people attractive from time to time. Some people tolerate the experience, remain faithful to their spouses, and move ahead. Others, like David, go on to the second cognitive error. Once he feels guilty, he is vulnerable to what some have called the "what-the-hell" phenomenon. He figures he has already sinned by finding a woman attractive, so he might as well go ahead and "sin big." He gets in the car and drives out of town.

After masturbating in his car, David uses the third cognitive error—blaming his behavior on his earlier normal experience; in this case, finding a woman attractive. Guilt and shame result. Sometimes to cope with his shame he might even blame the woman for looking too attractive or dressing in a certain way.

Once the dust settles, David's fourth cognitive error comes to him. "I will become more self-disciplined so this never happens again." So he becomes more rigid and self-critical of normal human experiences. He sets up inflexible, impossible standards for himself and others. Without knowing, he makes himself vulnerable for another fall in the near future.

The same cycle operates with a variety of behaviors. Consider some other examples:

Christine, the compulsive shopper

COGNITIVE ERROR 1: "It's bad to use a charge card." But there is a clearance sale at the department store and Christine has no cash with her. So she charges a blouse.

COGNITIVE ERROR 2: "I've already blown it by charging this blouse. I might as well enjoy myself." Christine quickly charges $300 in clothes.

COGNITIVE ERROR 3: "I knew it was a mistake to use my charge card!" She feels guilt and shame, and doesn't tell her husband about it until the bill comes.

COGNITIVE ERROR 4: "From now on, I will never use a charge card! Charge cards are evil." This works fine for a few weeks. Until the next clearance sale....

Paul, the angry parent

COGNITIVE ERROR 1: "A good father is never mad at his child."

Paul has told Brian four times to carry his plate into the kitchen and Brian still hasn't done it. He feels angry.

COGNITIVE ERROR 2: "I've already blown it by feeling this anger. Now he's going to pay!"

Paul screams at Brian and calls him a lazy slob.

COGNITIVE ERROR 3: "I should never have gotten angry."

Paul feels guilty, apologizes to Brian, and carries the plate to the kitchen himself.

COGNITIVE ERROR 4: "I will never get angry with Brian again."

Brian does the same thing the next night. Guess how Paul responds.

Brenda, the overeater

COGNITIVE ERROR 1: "I should never eat sugar. It makes me binge."

But don't those chocolate chip cookies look sensational! Brenda eats one.

COGNITIVE ERROR 2: "I've blown it now! Maybe another one or two won't hurt."

A dozen cookies later, Brenda's aching stomach reaches capacity.

COGNITIVE ERROR 3: "I knew sugar makes me binge. I never should have had the first one."

Guilt follows, and resolutions for the future.

COGNITIVE ERROR 4: "I will never have sugar again."

But those brownies sure smell good....

David, Christine, Paul, and Brenda all ended up losing their struggles in these examples. They first went astray by not allowing themselves to have normal human experiences. Since all of us have desires to eat, be angry, express sexuality, and own nice things (and these desires are not always evil), we can never completely kill the dark side. When we try we simply end up hiding our desires for pleasure underneath our approval-seeking glossy side. Soon we live in two worlds:

one we show to others and one we struggle to hide. Before long we give up on true authenticity and just hope others will think we are authentic (a glossy side desire).

Trying to kill Hyde doesn't work—desires for pleasure just come back stronger than ever when we try. Stevenson wrote of the dark side, "And when the attempt is made to cast it off, it but returns upon us with more unfamiliar and more awful pressure."

Having said this, let me quickly add that total abstinence is sometimes wise. For example, many believe they must abstain from alcohol to recover from an addiction. Others choose to tear up credit cards if they have a compulsive spending problem. This is fine, but eliminating the behavior does not necessarily deal with the underlying problems. The recovering alcoholic may develop other addictions. Compulsive spenders can spend a lot of money, even without credit cards. We must look deeper than the behavior itself.

What if David, Christine, Paul, and Brenda had tried a different strategy? What might have happened if Luke Skywalker left his weapons at the door of the cave as Yoda suggested? When we try to understand the source of our feelings rather than running from them or attacking them in fear, we have an opportunity to grow in wisdom and authenticity. Instead of condemning themselves for having normal feelings, the characters in these examples could have accepted the feelings and worked to manage them appropriately. When dealing with pleasure-seeking urges, the best principle is to manage the feelings rather than trying to eliminate them.

> DAVID: I am attracted to her. This is normal and I can manage these feelings responsibly. This may be affecting my counseling objectivity, so I'll discuss it with a friend and get some advice.

> CHRISTINE: Occasionally using a charge card is all right if I handle it responsibly. I'll buy the blouse I need and then put the card away.

> PAUL: Every father gets angry with his children from time to time. Brian is being irresponsible and it's okay for

him to know I am displeased. I can speak firmly in anger without losing control.

BRENDA: Sugar is not the real problem; eating too much is the problem. I can have one cookie, and then I'll stop.

•••

SELF-AWARENESS EXERCISE:

Having read the examples on David's sexual compulsion, Christine's shopping habits, Paul's anger, and Brenda's eating, reflect on your own life. Can you recognize these cognitive errors in any behavior you are trying to change? If so, look closely at cognitive error #1 and see if you can find a more realistic way to think about the situation. Since we can't kill the dark side, we must learn to live with and properly manage urges for pleasure. Sometimes we try to control Jekyll by calling on Hyde or control Hyde by calling on Jekyll. Neither strategy works very well.

•••

Fighting Hyde with Jekyll

I asked my daughter once what she should do if she broke a friend's toy. Her three-year-old mind spun quickly and she blurted, "Hide it." As adults, don't we have the same tendency? If we do something wrong, our first impulse is to hide it. Like Watergate conspirators, we so quickly ask ourselves, "How can I cover up this fault?" We fight Mr. Hyde by employing Dr. Jekyll.

Do any of the following thoughts sound familiar?

"A good person would never do something like I've just done."

"If others knew what I was really like, they would have nothing to do with me."

"If anyone finds out about this, my reputation will be ruined."

"This has to be my (our) secret. No one else can ever know."

These thoughts come from our desire to cover our faults, but they don't help us deal with the source of our problems. Sometimes the results are devastating.

Jan, an attractive thirty-year-old, enjoyed a successful career as an accountant for a large manufacturing company. Two years into her position she began noticing Tom, a friendly new coworker who whistled and grinned as she walked by his office each morning. Though she was married, Jan couldn't help feeling flattered, especially since Tom was handsome and popular around the office. As days passed Jan's embarrassed smile turned into a laugh, and then a pause at Tom's door to exchange office gossip or jokes. Soon their coffee breaks magically coincided, and Tom began sitting next to her in the staff lounge for lunch each day.

One afternoon, after other employees left the lounge to return to work, Tom and Jan lingered behind. Gingerly putting his hand on Jan's, Tom said, "You know, I really feel something for you. I'd like to get serious about this relationship."

Jan panicked. She knew an affair wouldn't be right, but she had the same attraction to Tom that he had to her. "I'm sorry—I just can't!" she said, and fled the lounge. She felt terrible and blamed herself for the situation: "Others will think I'm a terrible wife and a lousy employee if they find out what has happened." She couldn't talk with anyone because she feared their disapproval, so she decided to handle the situation herself. Thereafter, she avoided Tom's office on the way to hers, and took lunches alone. Still unable to get him out of her mind, she quit her job at the company and began looking for a new position elsewhere. But every change in her routine reminded her of her reason for change—Tom.

Several weeks later, Jan and her husband went to their first counseling session. During those intervening weeks, she had lost control. Convinced that she could no longer resist the temptation, she called Tom and told him that she was ready to leave her husband. A brief affair followed, but both Tom and Jan knew that it could never work. After considering suicide Jan drank herself to unconsciousness. Her husband found her and took her to the psychiatric ward at a nearby hospital. After she was discharged, Jan and her husband found a counselor.

Jan's dark side evoked the cognitive errors of the glossy side. Her desires for Tom were quickly followed by guilt, the glossy side condemning her for feeling attracted to someone other than her spouse. She skipped from the first cognitive error ("I shouldn't have these feelings") to the fourth ("I need to get out of this situation and then

I will be okay"). So she quit her job, but she hadn't dealt with the source of her problem, her attraction to Tom. Disaster followed.

Some things in life have to be worked through rather than avoided. As one songwriter put it, "No matter how fast I run I can never seem to get away from me." Changing jobs didn't help Jan because she hadn't yet learned to manage her feelings. Jan's guilt developed from her attraction for Tom. The more she was attracted, the more guilty she felt. Deciding to take another job was a way to cope with the guilt, but her dark side desires didn't go away.

Notice that Jan's battle was self-focused. She was so busy fighting Jekyll and Hyde, she had no time to look beyond her desires. Her dark side was interested in finding pleasure with Tom. Her glossy side was concerned about her reputation, and kept her from discussing the situation with a caring friend. By battling dark side and glossy side, Jan walled off her ability to pursue truth. She didn't even consider questions that her counselor later brought out:

- What can I learn about myself from this situation?
    What made me vulnerable to Tom's advances?
    Why did I keep this to myself?
    What needs was I hoping Tom would fulfill?
- What can I learn about marriage from this situation?
    Why is faithfulness important?
    In what ways do I better understand faithfulness now?
    How can I be a more faithful person, both sexually and nonsexually?
- How could this situation be handled differently if it happened again?
    What are the early warning signs?
    Who could I confide in before the situation got out-of-hand?
    How can I be more honest with myself and others?

Fighting Jekyll with Hyde

Lucretius warned, "Too much religion is apt to encourage evil." Just as dark side urges evoke the guilt of the glossy side, the unrealistic demands of the glossy side evoke the urges of the dark side. Thus, one self-focused desire fuels the other, and we try to fight Jekyll with Hyde.

Because he realized that unnecessary restrictions created unnecessary temptations, one biblical writer warned that extra rules, such as "do not touch" or "do not taste" are of "no value against fleshly indulgence." Often those exposed to the most severe rules become the most severe rebels.

The public failures of religious leaders have caused some to assume all televangelists are con artists after gullible donors. A closer look suggests their failures may relate to the Jekyll/Hyde battle and not to hypocrisy.

"Why? Why? I have asked myself that ten thousand times through ten thousand tears. Maybe Jimmy Swaggart has tried to live his entire life as though he was not human." When televangelist Jimmy Swaggart spoke these words to the public in 1988, they were lost in a swirl of emotion (he had just confessed to hiring a prostitute). But they may have been his most important words because they hint at the cause of Swaggart's transgression.

Maybe Jimmy Swaggart had tried to live his life as though he were not human. Maybe he thought his followers expected him to rise above human weakness. Maybe they did. Jekyll's messages were strong: "Appear perfect." "Show no faults." In the midst of such strong glossy side urges, dark side desires and resentments are stirred up, resulting in a secret life of sin. The glossy side evokes the dark side. And fighting Jekyll with Hyde doesn't work well; not for television evangelists and not for the rest of us either.

All the examples in this chapter have something in common: people struggling in private, feeling fearful or embarrassed to honestly confront their struggles and confide in a trustworthy friend. Hyde battles Jekyll. Jekyll battles Hyde. The days blur into weeks and months and years, and the battles remain. The guilt and shame and self-focus form a layer of storm clouds that linger like February in the Pacific Northwest. Authenticity requires self-understanding and trusting relationships with others. It can never happen in private. Authenticity is a team sport.

5

THE PERFECT DISGUISE

We all want to be authentic. But sometimes authenticity gets sacrificed for quick-fixes—styles of relating that only appear authentic. This chapter and the next describe two quick-fix obstacles to authenticity.

Remember both the Jekyll part and the Hyde part of one's personality play important roles. We could not function without them because we need some self-focus to survive. But too much of a good thing ceases to be good.

As discussed earlier, having the right amount of Dr. Jekyll allows us to be socially adept and interpersonally sensitive. Our desire for approval allows us to respond politely and attach appropriately to those around us. Without Dr. Jekyll, we would be socially insensitive—offensive, rude, and impolite. But when the Dr. Jekyll side gains too much power, people become consumed with perfection and addicted to approval.

Imagine you are in a political conversation with your neighbor who sees things differently than you do. You listen politely, but feel impatient as your neighbor insists her view is correct. Besides, you really want to get home and eat dinner. As your stomach growls for the tenth time, your neighbor says, "Come on in the house for a moment. I want to show you an editorial in the paper today." Choose your best response:

> RESPONSE 1: I think you're wrong, I'm hungry, and I'm going home. I don't care about the editorial.

RESPONSE 2: Thanks for that invitation, but I would like to get home for dinner now. We don't agree on this issue, but I will be happy to read the editorial later. RESPONSE 3: I would love to read the editorial. Your ideas are so enlightening to me.

The first response reflects too little social sensitivity. If you responded this way to your neighbor, you would be perceived as rude and cold. The second response is both honest and socially sensitive. If you chose the third response, you would be more concerned about your neighbor's approval than honesty. You would be yielding to Dr. Jekyll.

Yielding to Jekyll is a quick-fix. It may appear authentic to some, but life remains shallow and self-focused. Those yielding to Jekyll see authenticity as a political concept. They work to polish their outer layer so they appear sincere and authentic when talking with others. Sometimes they will admit to faults, but only when it will enhance their image as authentic people. They run the campaign trail of life, seeking popularity while denying their inner struggles and feelings. They often end up in a counselor's office because of empty, broken relationships and a lack of meaning in life.

Maintaining an image of perfection is painfully stressful. In my work I frequently learn of situations involving the immorality of public leaders, those who are often pressured into a self-marketing mentality because of the high expectations of those they lead. When their transgressions become known, they surprise everyone—spouses, close friends, colleagues. And often the one caught in deceit expresses relief: "I don't have to live this lie anymore."

How Does It Start?

It probably begins with our early desires to be attached to our caregivers and the childhood fear that we will be abandoned if we are naughty, needy, or weak.

Children spill milk, break dishes, and accidentally hurt playmates. To complicate this, they do not discriminate well between immoral acts and irresponsible acts. If they hear harsh judgment in response to their actions, they learn to hide all behaviors that have negative outcomes in order to remain attached to their caregivers. Punishing a child for accidental damage communicates that absolute perfection is the only acceptable standard. The child becomes convinced that every negative aspect of personality must be hidden, whatever the cost.

Perfection Grown Up

The drive for perfection doesn't end with childhood. The actors change, but the pressure remains. Self-marketing becomes even more important because social status, job security, and respect depend on it.

Social pressures reinforce the tendency to hide our inner struggles. When we see others in a social setting, we see what they want us to see. We rarely see their weaknesses unless revealed in a moment of frustration or extreme temptation. Sometimes we conclude that others have no weaknesses.

This increases our sense of aloneness and emptiness. When we look around and see the best parts of others, we assume that they don't have the struggles, sins, and temptations that we have. As a result we end up feeling dirty and evil. Ironically, others look at us, see our best qualities, and feel the same sense of inadequacy and emptiness. We've become so intent on marketing ourselves that we shut off the possibility of true intimacy and authenticity.

There are millions of people in our culture who have no intimate friends with whom they can be authentic and open. They carry the burden of others' expectations. They appear confident and strong on the outside, but the years of hiding have taken a toll, and they feel weak and vulnerable.

Why don't we just change? Why don't we just decide to show others how vulnerable and weak and tempted we are, hoping they will reciprocate? Because the risk seems too great. When someone dares to admit dark side desires, others often respond with the judgment and easy answers of the glossy side.

One Sunday a young man admitted a problem with anger at church. He acknowledged getting so angry that he wanted to throw things at family members. I appreciated his honesty, and headed his direction after the closing prayer. After contemplating his situation during the service, I wanted to respond. Perhaps our conversation would have gone like this.

MARK: I appreciate your honesty today. That must have been hard to talk about in front of this many people.

MAN: It was pretty hard to talk about, but I figure if I can't talk about my problems here, I can't talk about them anywhere.

MARK: I'm glad to hear that. Anger is one of those feelings we all identify with. I know I have my share and I don't always handle it well. Isn't it strange that family members can trigger anger more quickly than others?

MAN: Yeah, you would think we would be nicest to those we love the most, but it doesn't always work that way.

MARK: I'm not sure if I can help, but if I can, let me know. I would be glad to talk some more about this.

This conversation never happened, because by the time I reached him, he was already having another conversation with an elder in the church. It went something like this:

ELDER: I was sorry to hear about your problem.

MAN: Well, thanks. It was hard to talk about.

ELDER: What I find is that anger is a warning sign of my spiritual condition. When I get angry, I need to spend more time in prayer and Bible study.

MAN: Thanks. I'll give that a try.

After his conversation with the elder, the man had no interest in discussing it further with me or anyone else. Even if the elder's advice was right, it was insensitive timing. The elder said one thing, and the young man heard, "I am more spiritual than you so I don't have the same problems you have." The young man expressed a dark-side urge, making himself vulnerable, and the response was a quick answer that served to elevate the image of the advice-giver. The dark side of one evoked the glossy side of another.

Of course some people give glib replies not because they are seeking power, but because they don't know what else to say. Their good intent gets twisted into words that sound like an easy answer. Unfortunately, the desire to look good often drives others away and those with all the answers end up missing what they need most—intimate relationships with others.

It Doesn't Work

Yielding to Dr. Jekyll is a quick-fix that doesn't work. Sure, it relieved Dr. Jekyll who could lead his respectable life and hold his head high in the absence of Mr. Hyde, but the long-term results were harmful.

Conformity and Aloneness. Yielding to the glossy side simultaneously creates both conformity and aloneness. Externally, we conform to others because we long to fit in. But internally, we feel alone and empty.

In the movie *Taps* Timothy Hutton leads a group of adolescents who have decided to defend their military school from being closed by state authorities. When the boys find automatic weapons in the school arsenal, the tension builds. That night one boy slips over the school fence to escape the danger. The next morning, Hutton calls all the boys together and announces that anyone who wants to leave is free to go. The boys all stand at attention. No one moves. No one wants to be different! Finally, one brave student drops his rifle and walks conscientiously out the gate to safety. As he leaves, others begin filing out. A few at first, then dozens leave the hopeless cause and head instead for safety.

This scene clearly portrays the need for conformity. None of the boys wished to be the first to leave, but once one left, many left. No one wants to be different. We want to fit in with others. We stand to give an ovation even when the speaker wasn't that good, because everyone around us is standing. Yet as we conform with our behavior, we often feel alone in our personal struggles.

Shallow Relationships. When was the last time you confided your deepest inner pain with a friend whom you could trust with your darkest secrets? For some, it may have been yesterday or last week. For others, it was years ago during high school or college. Still others may never have had this kind of confiding relationship.

If your friend responded well, do you remember the exhilarating freedom of releasing that inner secret? Sharing inner pain lightens the burden of life and adds a bounce to one's stride.

But these kinds of authentic friendships are not easy to find, especially for those who cope with Jekyll/Hyde conflicts by hiding their inner struggles. Friends may abound—golfing buddies, football friends, biking partners—but intimacy is strangely absent. Many live in a world where they have squeezed out intimacy by keeping secrets and tried to replace true intimacy with unusual accomplishment, popularity, or financial success.

Vulnerability to Evil. When temptations are banished to the dungeon of inner secrecy, they gain strength and can eventually dominate the human personality. Only when they are brought to the light of day can they be managed properly.

Those recovering from alcohol or drug abuse, sexual compulsions, and eating disorders recognize that hiding a problem makes it grow stronger. When you admit a problem to others, you can manage it better.

• •

SELF-AWARENESS EXERCISE:

Write down your most persistent, troubling fault. Now imagine a front-page story on your local newspaper describing your fault. On an embarrassment scale from 0 to 10, this would be a 10. Now imagine that 100 people know about your fault. How bad would that be on the embarrassment scale? Now imagine that 25 people know about your fault. How bad would that be? Now imagine that just one person, a caring friend, knows about your fault. How bad would that be? Maybe not as bad as it seemed before doing this exercise.

• •

If I ran an electronics repair shop, I would encourage my employees to take the covers off VCRs before trying to repair them. Maneuvering tools and integrated circuits through little doors the size of VHS tapes would not improve employee satisfaction or customer service. If anyone were foolish enough to try fixing a VCR this way, I would insist, "Take the cover off so you can see what you are working on."

It's hard to make the repairs necessary in our lives when the problems are covered by layers of reputation and self-protection. Though it's often painful to expose our problems to the light of day, it's the only way to break the powerful hold of approval-seeking. Authenticity requires light.

6

IF IT FEELS GOOD . . .

Bumper stickers are good thermometers for the climate of society. Sometime between the peace stickers of the sixties and the anti-government, anti-everything stickers of the nineties, it was common to see the adage, "If it feels good, do it." It's an interesting philosophy, but it doesn't take a great mind to realize that it isn't very practical. One man displaying such a bumper sticker was rammed from behind while waiting at a traffic light. The driver of the assaulting car shrugged and casually remarked, "It felt good."

Just as we can have too little or too much emphasis on Dr. Jekyll, the same is true for Mr. Hyde. The pleasure-focused Hyde plays an essential role in personality, but it requires delicate balance.

Three accountants leave the office building on Friday afternoon, get in their cars and contemplate the upcoming weekend. Each has a different set of thoughts.

> PAT: I really should get those ledgers done before Monday morning. If I work hard these next two days, I may get them done.

> TERRY: There is a lot of work to be done, but it's important to take some time to relax also. I'll work a bit tomorrow morning and go to the park with my family.

> JESSE: Friday is finally here! It's time to party, party, party. The deadline can wait.

We can invest too little in pleasure, as Pat may be guilty of in this example. Pleasure plays an important role in life; we need to have fun from time to time. Terry is working to balance pleasure with responsibility. Jesse overemphasizes pleasure, yielding to Mr. Hyde. If it feels good, Jesse will do it—and pay the price later.

If It Feels Good

After some initial battles with Jekyll and Hyde, some decide to abandon traditional morality and seek pleasure. If it feels good, they do it. They give up the glossy side, and allow Mr. Hyde to take over. Seeking pleasure is good, but when the desire for pleasure becomes the main theme of one's life, it causes problems. Just as a drug addict seeks narcotics at any cost, those addicted to pleasure seek self-satisfaction at any cost. They avoid responsibility and rationalize immorality in the race for fun. Mr. Hyde takes over.

Yielding to Hyde is another ineffective quick-fix to resolve the tensions between Jekyll and Hyde. It appears as authenticity to some, because there is very little struggle between Jekyll and Hyde. Hyde dominates. But there is a problem. Long-standing relationships require more than pleasure. They require commitment, faithfulness, altruism, and honesty. So as people race through life pursuing pleasure, relationships wither and fade away. The rewards of pursuing pleasure stale with time, and so does the illusion of authenticity.

If You Can't Be Good Enough

"Don't try." This is a common attitude of those yielding to Hyde. They have given up the struggle and let pleasure rule.

Linda quietly contemplated my question about childhood, then began describing her early years with some hesitation and awkwardness. I almost missed the crucial element of her revelation because I was expecting a horrific story of sexual abuse. Whenever she handled her genitals as a child, her father became outraged and told her that good girls don't do that. He apparently didn't know that virtually all children explore and play with their genitals during preschool years, with or without their parents' permission. Linda was no exception, but because of her father's punitive reactions, she learned to be more cautious. Sexual exploration became a private "sin" for Linda. Because she was a normal child, she found pleasure in self-manipulation, all the time experiencing guilt because of her father's words.

Linda's sexual behavior remained a central theme as she grew: playing doctor with children in the neighborhood, extreme promiscuity in high school and college, repeated cohabitation with men as an adult. She viewed the world in sexual terms and seemed to have little control over her sexual behavior.

Once Linda broke into tears in my office. "I don't want to be bad", she sobbed, "all I ever wanted to do was to make people happy." Linda faced an emotional dilemma. She wanted to please her father, to act like good girls act, but she just couldn't be good enough. She stopped trying, but held on to her profound feelings of guilt.

Linda's home was characterized by rigid rules. She couldn't watch television because it might have a negative influence. Anger was not allowed. The rigidity of her home did not prevent the struggle between Jekyll and Hyde, it only made it private. In the fertile soil of secrecy, Linda's dark side grew magnificently. It burst into prominence during her teenage years and had remained in control ever since.

Well-meaning parents try to protect their children from the influences of evil. But the results backfire when the expectations are excessive. Unrealistic expectations communicate to children that having a dark side is unacceptable. If it feels good, *don't* do it. When those children experience inevitable temptations, they cannot go to their parents because they fear punishment or verbal condemnation. Coping with the dark side becomes a private battle.

How many teenagers leave home and go crazy pursuing pleasure? It doesn't happen suddenly. Those dark side urges have been growing for years but because they have not been acknowledged in the home, the child has developed no resources to manage them. Independence doesn't create new temptations, it only allows existing temptations to be experienced openly.

· ·

SELF-AWARENESS EXERCISE:

Finish this sentence, "Life should be _____." Come up with several responses. After each of your responses, write a sentence describing the evidence you have that life should be that way. Our assumptions about life shape the way we interpret our experiences and plan for the future. And some assumptions make us vulnerable to yielding to Hyde.

· ·

Life Should Be Fair and Fun

We confuse fair and fun frequently. "I work hard but can never save enough for that new boat or sports car. It just isn't fair." Or, "I can't spend the rest of my life with my wife because I'm in love with another woman. It just wouldn't be fair to me or my wife." You see the pattern: "It's not fair if life isn't pleasurable."

In our culture of luxuries and entertainment, many assume a life without pleasure is a pointless existence. So they seek pleasure, often neglecting to explore deeper values in life. Yielding to Hyde is the result.

A careful look at the assumption that life should be fair and fun helps us see ourselves and our world more accurately. Carefully ponder how fair is the fate of a newborn Ethiopian child or a South African black citizen. Speaking of fun would seem callous to a Haitian mother whose child is slowly starving. The assumption that life should be fair and therefore fun is not intrinsically true.

Me, Myself, and I

Another common belief is that we need to look out for ourselves first. The heroes in today's movies stand up and rebel against authority. The good guys are the ones that break the rules. We have lost our awareness of community and mutual responsibility. In a survey, high school students were asked, "Where do you look for truth?" The number one response was, "I look to myself." Authority has been replaced with the sovereignty of the individual.

One of the leading behavior therapy textbooks gives a three-pronged definition of assertiveness. Assertive behavior is:

1. The straightforward expression of thoughts and feelings;
2. Socially appropriate;
3. That which takes into account the feelings of others.

Somewhere between the textbook and the popular ideas about assertiveness, the second and third parts of this definition have been omitted. Assertiveness has been contaminated and misinterpreted in our individualistic society to give license for selfishness. To many, assertiveness means, "I do whatever I want."

Hyde Falls Flat

Yielding to Hyde is a quick fix. It seems to snatch us out of the grips of our struggles, at least at first. But soon it becomes confusing and frustrating. As one formerly promiscuous client put it, "I've been down that road, and it's not what it seems."

Many pleasure-seeking behaviors are self-destructive. By participating in them, we defeat ourselves. People abuse alcohol to escape problems or to enjoy social occasions. Liver disease, memory deficits, loss of inhibition, and traffic deaths remind us that alcohol does more than its abusers intend. Their efforts to escape problems have only created new, more serious, problems. Others eat excessively to escape the loneliness they feel. Soon they despise themselves and feel lonelier with each passing year. Others seek happiness through possessions. Like the bumper sticker proclaims, "The one with the most toys wins!" But accumulating things creates more demands for income, more work-related pressures, and soon people become so busy making a living that there is no time left for living.

Bob, a married man, found himself attracted to Christine, a coworker. Falling in love is fun, and for a time Bob's depression, for which he was in counseling, was reduced after meeting Christine. He felt energetic and alive again. Though he firmly believed having an affair would be morally wrong, he seemed unable to explore the consequences of having an affair. He could produce the glossy side stance ("I shouldn't have an affair"), but couldn't view the new relationship from a truth-centered perspective (he couldn't express why he shouldn't have an affair). Bob decided to have an affair. Jekyll and Hyde battled and Mr. Hyde won. Several months later Bob stood in the midst of the rubble he created. Broken relationships with his wife, his children, and Christine told the story. His depression returned stronger than ever. Bob was his own victim.

Why do we engage in self-destructive behaviors? Because we don't carefully evaluate consequences. Bob refused to view his dilemma from a truth-centered perspective because he was so invested in the self-focused Jekyll-Hyde battle. If any of us could have listened to Bob's thoughts, we would have heard something like this:

Hyde: Go for it! It feels great to be in love.

Jekyll: You can't have an affair, it is wrong!

Hyde: Don't worry about it, just enjoy yourself.

Jekyll: The Bible says not to commit adultery.

Hyde: You can't be perfect all the time. Enjoy!

Truth-centered perspective(counselor in this case):

Let's consider the consequences.

Hyde and Jekyll: Shut up and stay out of this!

The battle raged for several weeks before the dark side won. As Bob soon discovered, yielding to Mr. Hyde is self-defeating. The glamour of sin is attractive, but its consequences are destructive.

Quick fixes to the Jekyll/Hyde struggle don't work. Jekyll and Hyde both keep us self-focused, but authenticity requires us to move beyond our selfish desires for pleasure and approval.

PART II
PRINCIPLES FOR AUTHENTIC LIVING

7

HAVE A CLEAR SET OF VALUES

The Jekyll-Hyde struggle can never be completely fixed or avoided, but we can significantly reduce the problems we experience. In this next section we'll consider seven principles that can help us learn to manage life's struggles and to live authentic, wholesome lives.

The first three principles (chapters 9-11) have to do with personal understanding and self-awareness. The next three principles (chapters 12-14) relate to interpersonal awareness, the need for authenticity in the presence of others. The final principle (chapter 15) takes a bold look at grace—we can be loved and accepted without having to earn love.

The first principle for personal authenticity is that we must have a clear set of values. Years ago someone titled a book, "If You Don't Know Where You're Going, You'll Probably End Up Somewhere Else." We need a clear set of values to point out directions in the midst of moral and social confusion.

Consider three examples. Look for ways values guide the main characters' thoughts and behavior.

John is verbally aggressive with Sally and has been throughout the fifteen years of their marriage. When Sally shows her displeasure, John denies any wrongdoing and blames Sally for not being more submissive. Sally has learned ways to cope, however. For example, she takes the charge card to the shopping mall and spends large amounts of money. When the bill comes the following month, John is mad but he really can't do anything to stop Sally. Sally is convinced that the problems in the marriage are all John's fault. John is convinced the problems are all Sally's.

Brenda and Jane are intimate friends. They take time away from busy schedules each week to spend time together. They share their deepest fears, successes, and faults with one another and each could literally trust the other with her life.

When Chris stands up and shares in church, she has a way of bringing out guilt in others. Last week, she talked about how she gets up at 5:30 every morning to have personal devotions for an hour before work. She talks about how God's love helps her to be kind and gentle with others. Her children listen to her speak in church and know she is not telling the truth.

Each of these examples points out the role values play in our lives. First, think about the values John and Sally have. They both have a commitment to their marriage—they have persisted in theirs for fifteen years. John believes in expressing his feelings to Sally, but seems to lack awareness of his own part in their troubles. He doesn't tell himself the truth about his own faults and he isn't taking responsibility for his anger. At the same time, Sally values peace. She works to avoid conflict. But she gets revenge too. She gets back at John and balances the power in the relationship by overusing the charge card. She doesn't tell herself the truth either and won't acknowledge her reckless spending as a problem. Both John and Sally value self-protection. They lie to themselves to stay protected.

Brenda and Jane value honesty with one another and they value their relationship. They discuss their deepest feelings and hurts in life. They discuss their faults together. By being honest with one another, they become more honest with themselves. They tell each other the truth.

Chris values approval. She wants others to know how spiritual she is. Privately, her life might be quite different than it appears on Sunday morning. She spends so much time perfecting the glossy side because the darker side of her nature scares her so profoundly. She lies to herself about her deepest fears and desires and ends up presenting a false self to others.

In our contemporary cultural climate, you may be expecting this chapter to say something like this: "It doesn't matter so much what your values are, but you need to *know* the values that guide your life."

In one sense, I like the flexibility and acceptance communicated in such a concept, but it's not what you'll find in this chapter. Both are important: *knowing* one's values *and* the values themselves. One of the tragedies of contemporary culture is the belief that we look inside ourselves to determine what our values should be. History provides ample evidence that some values are better than others. We need to be honest about what our values are while working to live by the most honorable and globally effective values. Although there are many worthy values, we will consider only three in this chapter: honesty, intimacy, and faithfulness. I choose these three because authentic relationships occur only in their presence.

The Value of Honesty

The value of honesty with ourselves and others is seen in all these examples. Before we can know our deepest values, we must be honest with ourselves. Before we can move away from self and toward truth, we need to value personal honesty. The poet John Masefield put it this way:

> Man with his burning soul
> Has but an hour of breath
> To build a ship of
> Truth in which his soul may sail
> Sail on the sea of death
> For death takes toll
> Of beauty, courage, youth,
> Of all but Truth.

Shakespeare penned the famous words, "To thine own self be true." Honesty is a starting point for a discussion of values, because only when we honestly know ourselves (truth-focused) can we know what we cherish.

Because truth is painful, we protect ourselves from it by constructing layers of heavy emotional armor that psychologists call defense mechanisms. Although we can never hope to strip away all the defenses, authenticity requires us to admit the defenses are there and to do what we can to look beyond them.

· ·

SELF-AWARENESS EXERCISE:

Think of a conflict you have with another person—maybe a spouse, a family member, a former friend, or a coworker. Now write a one paragraph description of how you contributed to the problem. Most of us could skillfully craft a paragraph describing the other person's faults, but when we write about our own faults it is more difficult because of our defense mechanisms.

· ·

Though we sometimes use a guise of honesty to criticize others ("I'm only saying it because it's true"), being honest with and about ourselves is much more difficult. It's easier to defend ourselves against criticism than to look for truth in the midst of criticism. Imagine your spouse saying, "Honey, I don't think you're spending enough time with the kids." Most of us respond defensively to such criticism:

"You don't know how much responsibility I have at work right now."

"I spend a lot of time with the kids compared to other parents I know."

"You need to think about your own life instead of criticizing mine."

Wouldn't it be great if we could get beyond the defenses, be honest with ourselves, and see the truth in what others tell us, even if they don't say it perfectly? Wouldn't it be great to see ourselves honestly, as others who know us well see us?

One of my blind spots has been my hopeless idealism—believing the world should proceed according to my schedule and values. I am learning to confront my idealism because I finally started listening when Lisa discussed it with me (after dozens of times when I didn't listen). And with God's grace and the patience of family and close friends, I am changing.

The value of honesty requires us, in the words of John Masefield, to build our ship of truth. We might say our ships are vehicles for exploring ourselves—going beyond the layers of defense mechanisms to the frontier of personal truth. Honesty is a prerequisite to authenticity.

The Value of Intimacy

Because authenticity occurs in the context of relationships, authentic people recognize the value of being close to others. Our tendency is to overrate or undervalue relationships. We overrate relationships when we imply they are most important thing in life. Many things are of crucial importance in life, only one of which is healthy relationships. We undervalue relationships when we assume they are disposable or optional.

Disposing of relationships is a natural human tendency, not because our friends aren't perfect—we can handle that—but because our friends cause us to look at our own imperfections. Seeing our own flaws can overwhelm us. It's easier to "dump" the relationship and start over with someone who thinks we are wonderful. For those who persist, long-term relationships force personal awareness and greater authenticity.

••

SELF-AWARENESS EXERCISE:

Try another experiment. Think of a person with whom you have a broken relationship. It may be the same person you thought of when thinking of a personal conflict earlier in this chapter. Now write a paragraph about how this other person perceives you. Reread the paragraph and see if you can find some truth in the other person's perspectives.

••

Intimate relationships can help us see ourselves honestly. Psychotherapy is one such relationship, though it is contaminated by its one-sided nature and the fact that it is often purchased. Research on psychotherapy is quite clear about the value of the relationship. The specific techniques the therapist uses seem to be less important than the trusting, confiding nature of the relationship. In the context of a good therapeutic relationship, people see themselves more honestly and begin to deal with problems differently.

This is a lesson I am still learning as a college professor. I may spend hours polishing a brilliant (to me, at least) lecture and have less impact on a student's life than I have in a fifteen minute chat after class. In fact, it's sometimes difficult to move away from my computer, where I'm preparing my lecture, to attend to a student who has stopped by to say hello. Both the lecture and the relationship are important, but the greatest potential for honest, authentic communication can be found in the relationship.

Relationships that foster authenticity are comprised of two or more people who care about one another and are willing to be honest. Relationships that foster authenticity cannot be manipulative. If a relationship is a means to an end, a status symbol, a way to be perceived as popular, smart, or chic, it will not help its participants become more authentic.

The quick fixes—giving in to Jekyll's glossiness or yielding to Hyde's dark desires—are ways of avoiding an honest look at ourselves. Unfortunately, they also push away the possibility of healthy relationships. The one who is yielding to Jekyll by denying temptation and weakness may have the respect of others and may have many casual relationships, but is fearful to let people close enough to see the truth. Jekyll becomes a defense mechanism to shield oneself from the temptation lurking inside. Yielding to Hyde, pursuing pleasure with wild abandon, may lead to numerous relationships, but not necessarily healthy relationships that lead to personal honesty.

The Value of Faithfulness

There is no better place to learn faithfulness than in the context of long-standing relationships. Those married for thirty years know more about faithfulness than those married for three. Those who walk with a friend through cancer treatment know more about faithfulness than those who have never faced similar tragedy.

Faithfulness cannot be learned without drudgery, routine, boredom, and toil. Commitment must stand the test of time before it can be called faithfulness. When we're convinced of another's faithfulness, we can risk being authentic with them.

We learn faithfulness in the routines of life. If life on the edge is exciting, life in the middle, with its ruts and routines, forces us to stand in the same place long enough to fully test our character. The routines of life are where we learn to be faithful to God, though our questions about God may seem more ominous than before. And this is where we begin to understand our marriage vows because we've better learned the cost of faithfulness through the minor or major trials that come with marriage. We learn to be faithful to our children as we deal with their needs day after day. We learn to be faithful to our friends. These are the ones who help us dismantle our defenses, our emotional armor that starts wearing thin in the middle years of our lives. These are the ones who are closest to us and stay with us to help us accept the ugliness and appreciate the beauty that remains after the defenses are gone.

Faithfulness can't be rushed and it won't always be fun, but faithfulness is a value that guides us through life's storms.

Authenticity requires us to know our values. It's a step away from self and toward truth. Let's work to value honesty, intimacy, and faithfulness.

8

DEVELOP SKILLS OF SELF-AWARENESS

I remember walking through the school playground as a child and suddenly being knocked over. After a few groggy seconds, I realized I had been hit in the head by a line drive in a softball game (strange—the ball didn't seem soft). At the time, I blamed the batter for hitting it so hard and so far. Now I ask, why was I strolling through left field without noticing where I was? I lacked self-awareness.

Those caught in the grip of the Jekyll/Hyde syndrome often describe something similar. They stroll along life's way and suddenly get knocked down by temptation. At first they blame others—spouse, employer, child, friend, lover, parent—but soon they realize the problem was caused by a basic lack of self-awareness. When they needed self-understanding, they focused on the desires of Jekyll or Hyde instead.

Self-awareness helps us appraise ourselves and our situations honestly. With self-awareness, we avoid strolling through left field. Without it, we get knocked down by surprise.

Masters of Disguise

A great impostor throughout his life, Fred Demara took on the identity of a Trappist monk, a Latin teacher, a cancer researcher, a military surgeon, and a psychology professor. Actually he was a high school dropout. Deciding against becoming an actor, he commented that acting seemed "too artificial." Demara spent much of his life searching for identity, never embracing who he was in reality. He was a master of disguise.

In more subtle ways, we are all masters of disguise. One way to shield ourselves from our faults is to find the same faults in others. Freud called it **projection**. A colleague once told me of an irate woman who called the police department, reporting that young people were driving too fast in her neighborhood. The police promptly followed up and issued their first ticket. Surprisingly, the woman making the report received the citation. Her criticism of the young drivers in her neighborhood reflected her own struggles with impulse control.

Denial is refusing to perceive negative aspects of ourselves. Alcoholics often refuse to admit to a drinking problem until they are forced to by painful circumstances. Students report they are late to class because their alarm didn't go off, rather than dealing with the reality that they turned off the alarm and went back to sleep. Politicians sometimes emphatically deny charges of wrongdoing, only to be publicly embarrassed when more evidence emerges. NBA players deny their fouls by glaring at and bickering with the referee.

Rationalization is attempting to prove a behavior is justifiable by producing well-reasoned arguments. One might reason, "It's okay to cheat on my taxes because the government wastes so much money anyway—having a few less dollars to spend on nuclear weapons won't hurt them." Self-focused motives can easily be disguised in costumes of rationality.

Projection, denial, and rationalization are examples of ways we disguise the truth to protect ourselves. They are obstacles to self-awareness.

••

SELF-AWARENESS EXERCISE:

Think of a major mistake or wrongdoing in your life (past or present). Can you see ways you disguised the truth using projection, denial, or rationalization? Try writing a confronting letter to yourself suggesting ways you could have been more honest and self-aware.

••

Steps to Self-awareness

Rather than walling off Dr. Jekyll or Mr. Hyde, we can open the doors to both. We can accept our urges for pleasure and approval as part of who we are, yet balance the self-focus of Jekyll and Hyde with our ability to look for truth, to see a bigger picture beyond our selfish desires.

How does one open the doors to Jekyll and Hyde and become self-aware? Here are a few ideas.

Expect normal desires. Defenses are triggered by desires. For example, I might have a fleeting desire to play golf on Monday morning instead of going to work, and I feel immediate guilt. If yielding to Jekyll was my inclination, I might tell myself that good people don't ever struggle with the temptation to play golf instead of working and that I am surely the biggest flake of all time. If I embrace Hyde's desire for pleasure, I might persuade myself that I need the leisure time and wouldn't be able to work anyway so I might as well play golf.

Feeling guilty for having normal desires is unproductive. Desires are not wrong until they give birth to evil. If, instead of feeling guilty, I acknowledge and accept my desire to play golf, I can gain self-awareness. I might affirm the value of work and go to the office for the right reasons. Or, if my job allows, I might decide my deadlines aren't as important as I think and go play golf. Remember, desires themselves are not evil. Spontaneously doing something "crazy" can be a wonderful experience that adds to mental and spiritual health. Deciding at the last minute to go to the beach for the weekend, choosing the more expensive dress just because it looks better, and selecting the lasagna instead of the diet plate can all be appropriate in some situations. To live life denying all desires is not the goal.

Similarly, desires for approval are healthy in mild doses. The opinions of others keep us socially appropriate. Desires can add joy to life as we accept them as part of ourselves. But like that softball in the school playground, we need to know desires are coming so we can handle them appropriately.

Identify emotions. Emotions are our biological motivators. When we feel afraid, we leave the situation. When angry, we assert the rights of others or ourselves. When happy, we find others to help us celebrate. Emotions keep us going.

If we are to understand ourselves accurately, we need to understand the emotions that motivate us. But understanding emotions can be difficult for several reasons.

First, many emotions are buried beneath layers of shame and childhood pain. Consider the following situations, all of which cause children to bury their feelings.

- Joe was raised in a devoutly religious home, but was incorrectly taught that anger is always sinful. Whenever he expressed anger, he was punished.
- Alicia was sexually abused as a child. She had feelings of shame, guilt, and despair but couldn't tell anyone because she feared what would happen to her and her abuser.
- Karen was insulted and shamed throughout childhood. Her earliest memories are of rejection. Ironically, she doesn't feel anything as she recalls these memories. Her feelings seem distant and faint.

As adults, Joe, Alicia, and Karen lack self-awareness because they cannot recognize their feelings accurately. Joe's major obstacle to knowing his feelings is labeling some emotions acceptable and others (e.g. anger) unacceptable. He feels guilty or shameful for experiencing anger, so he denies his anger and instead feels depressed.

Alicia and Karen lack awareness of their feelings because they learned to divorce their feelings from their experiences. When children confront feelings too painful to bear, they pretend the feelings aren't there. In adulthood the feelings start to emerge, bringing with them the painful memories from the past. The answer is not getting rid of the feelings—that's what the child tried earlier in life. The answer is accepting the feelings and working toward greater self-awareness.

Laugh. Being able to laugh at ourselves fosters self-awareness and self-acceptance. Sometimes we need a break from taking ourselves so seriously!

Think about how seriously we take sports. We pay millions of dollars to people who can hit a little ball a long way, or throw a bigger ball into a basket, or kick a funny-looking ball through a goal post.

And if our team doesn't win, we're ready to fire the coach or yell at the kids. One man got so upset that he threw his television out the window (which was closed). And if our team does win, we throw parties and have parades. As much as I love sports, it all seems pretty weird!

••

SELF-AWARENESS EXERCISE:

Think of a strange trait you have, discuss it with someone who knows you well, and try to find the humor in it. Rather than feeling shameful or embarrassed by your peculiarity, laughing at yourself helps you accept it as part of what makes you unique.

••

Pursue friendships. Seeing ourselves through the eyes of others helps us know ourselves better. As the writer of Proverbs stated, "Iron sharpens iron, so one [person] sharpens another."

One benefit of intimate friendship is that it allows us to share our struggles with someone who cares. My five-year-old daughter once suggested a way to share a Lifesaver. "I suck it for a while, then you suck it for a while, then I suck it some more…." Although a disgusting way to share Lifesavers, her model is useful for sharing struggles. Discussing our struggles with another makes them seem smaller just as a communal Lifesaver becomes smaller and smaller.

Measuring ourselves against Jekyll-like standards produces profound aloneness. "No one experiences the desires I do." "I am the worst of all sinners." Self-awareness can't be obtained in the midst of such self-condemnation, but disclosing struggles to others helps us realize our desires are manageable and often normal.

Of course indiscriminate self-disclosure can be dangerous. If self-disclosure is met with judgment or criticism, self-awareness is hindered. Let me show you what I mean.

Wanda is becoming self-aware. She is recognizing her desires and attempting to deal with them wisely. While feeling particularly lonely one day, Wanda finds herself in front of the refrigerator finishing her third piece of cheesecake. She ponders the connection, rests her head on her palms as she sits down at the kitchen table. "Could it be," she wonders, "that my eating problem is related to loneliness?" Rather than feeling guilty, she attempts to understand herself better by contemplating her recent weight gain, feelings of loneliness, and her compulsive eating.

Wanda makes an appointment with a counselor who specializes in eating disorders and enthusiastically tells her husband, Jon, when he arrives home that evening. Jon doesn't respond well.

"You had three pieces of cheesecake! You're already twenty pounds heavier than you were last year. What are you thinking of? Now you're going to spend money going to a counselor. I can tell you the problem—you're eating too much!" Jon has reacted to Wanda's self-disclosure by resorting to condemnation and easy answers.

Jon's reaction could push Wanda away from self-awareness. She might agree with Jon and try to stay away from the counselor and the refrigerator, but her problems will remain and eventually she will come back to the refrigerator. Once that happens, she will feel like a failure and her problems may worsen. Alternatively, she might disagree strongly with Jon's reactivity, pull away from him and become lonelier than ever.

Self-disclosure is appropriate, but choosing someone who will not overreact to the disclosure is important. It is important to recognize limits in self-disclosure. Wanda might have done better to mention the counselor to Jon without talking about the three pieces of cheesecake. She then could have mentioned the cheesecake to her counselor or another close friend if it seemed appropriate.

When self-disclosure doesn't evoke criticism, self-awareness is enhanced. In the best relationships both persons can disclose secrets without evoking judgment in the other. We can see ourselves best through the eyes of others.

9

DIRECT YOUR PASSION

Passion often underlies the Jekyll-Hyde struggle. When passions are misdirected or get out of control, people end up yielding to their dark sides. A typical way to cope with Hyde is trying to kill passion. Those who don't succeed in pushing back their passions sometimes end up struggling to balance a public life with a hidden private life. Those who successfully push back their passions may be worse off—they live as moral automatons plodding through life with rigid boundaries and defenses, being content to criticize others and long for the good old days that never were. When their efforts fail and passion peeks through, they become more determined than before to push it back again.

Denial of passion is fundamentally misdirected and carries the risk of emotional and spiritual atrophy. Indeed, many of the most orthodox believers in religious traditions are the most spiritually withered because they have cut off passion.

I must be careful not to overstate this. It is important that we control and direct our passions. A life of selfish pursuits often leads to moral and emotional bankruptcy. But if we deny our passion along with our selfish will, we end up spiritually bankrupt.

I think of a colleague whom I have long respected. He is a passionate person and he allows his passion to energize his life. Yes, he struggles with hidden desires—I've heard him speak of his addiction to food several times. But his passion also drives him to live out his beliefs. He doesn't just talk about peace, he travels overseas and works for peace. He doesn't just talk about simplicity, he lives a simple life so he can give his money to those who need it more than he does. I long for the kind of passion he has.

I think of five young men committed to their Christian beliefs and to the goal of telling others throughout the world about God's love. These five men of passion went to minister to a tribe in Ecuador, though they knew of the tribe's reputation as savage headhunters. All five were killed. It hardly seems like a happy ending. Passion is not safe.

But passion is contagious. Rachel Saint, sister of one of the five martyrs; Elisabeth Elliot, wife of another; and other relatives went back to Ecuador to show love and mercy rather than revenge. The murderers of those five missionaries became devout Christians living in a now peaceful community. It all happened because five men and several of their relatives refused to deny their passion.

The problem is not too much passion, it is misdirected passion. Like those missionaries in Ecuador, we all need passion that is directed toward something greater than ourselves. We need a mission.

A counseling client of mine suggested writing a mission statement for his life. We went through several steps as he came up with his mission statement. I liked the idea and the effects on his life, so I tried it myself. Here are the steps I went through:

Step 1: Personal Reflection

An effective mission comes from our inner passions and longings. But life gets so busy that it's difficult to see passions and longings accurately. We so easily end up living life by deadlines and expectations, from the outside in, rather than by vision, from the inside out. And after years of living by those deadlines and expectations, it's sometimes difficult to see anything else. Vision gets crowded out by outside demands.

The antidote, of course, is quiet time for personal reflection. It sounds so simple, but experience tells us it's not. Most of us have only a few minutes a day when we're not working, talking, or being entertained. Personal reflection gets squeezed out by external pressures.

SELF-AWARENESS EXERCISE:

Next time you're able to find time alone, try thinking and writing about the following questions. Your thoughts and words will help clarify your passions and deep inner longings.

1. What makes my heart break? (Look for the events and circumstances in life that touch you most deeply.)
2. What thrills me the most? (Write about the events that have given you a sense of energy and enthusiasm.)
3. How do others describe my best qualities?

This exercise will point people in different directions. Some will find they are most moved by ideas of significance. They love reading, thinking, and talking about ideas and concepts. Others, like the five missionaries who went to Ecuador, will find themselves compelled to help relieve human suffering. Others enjoy the challenge of organization or leadership.

Too often we assume others should be like us. Many devotional and inspirational talks across our country could be succinctly summarized: "Your passion should be the same as my passion." Our passions lead us in different directions, but each direction is important.

Let's celebrate our passions and our differences. They energize and direct us through difficult times, allow us to reach beyond ourselves, and remind us how much we need one another.

Step 2: Get Another Perspective

As suggested earlier, the best way to gain insight is through the eyes of another. Try another exercise to gain some additional insight.

SELF-AWARENESS EXERCISE:

Schedule some time with a close friend with the goal of discussing your mission. Describe to your friend what you are doing, then ask several questions:

1. If I worked for you, what kind of job would you have me doing? Why? (Look for your strengths in what your friend tells you.)

2. What do I get the most enthused about in life? (Your friend may have learned some things about you that you don't know by watching you react to various situations.)

3. If I didn't have to earn a living or support a family, what do you suppose I would do with my time? (Let your friend describe what you might do if your were freed to pursue your mission full-time.)

••

I'm not suggesting that people should change jobs, although that occasionally happens with the insight people gain in self-discovery. For most, it is more realistic to find ways of expressing their mission right where they are. I'll give some examples.

• Ron works as a janitor and has a mission for helping those in need. He and some coworkers make sandwiches and take them to the inner city on Saturday nights to brighten the day for many homeless.

• Jenny is a banker who is drawn to contemplating complex ideas. Each day she observes her customers and their differing ways of life, and she writes in a journal, exploring her thoughts and feelings and trying to better understand human nature.

• Lynn works as a homemaker and loves tasks of creative organization. She not only uses these skills at home, but also chairs a planning committee for her church.

Once people define their mission, they find ways to live out their passions at work and at home. Self-awareness frees us to do what thrills us and serve others at the same time.

Step 3: Write a Mission Statement

"Your mission is to boldly go where no one has gone before." Taken by itself, this is an absurd mission, but for most Baby Boomers, it reminds us of a specific television series. We picture the Starship Enterprise bursting into unknown space. We think of Captain Kirk kissing a different alien on each show, Mr. Spock's ears, the funny uniforms they all wore, and Mr. Scott's accent. It demonstrates how a single statement can trigger a cascade of emotions and memories and direct our thinking. A good mission statement does this.

Our mission comes from understanding ourselves, our values, and our passions. But a mission statement not only describes us, it also energizes us, directing and focusing our behavior, thoughts, and reactions, allowing us to be authentic rather than settling for counterfeit spirituality.

In writing a mission statement, keep several things in mind.

Keep it short. Most of us have a long mental list of goals and objectives in our lives: spend quality time with the children, be a responsible and productive employee, express love to my spouse, finish a degree, save for retirement, fix up the house, eat lowfat foods, exercise regularly, develop good friendships, and so on. All of these need not be included in an effective mission statement. Ideally, try to keep your mission statement to one sentence that can be memorized easily. Once memorized, it can be carried with you mentally wherever you go.

Keep it focused. Life has so many facets and moves by so rapidly that it's easy for it to become a blur. How can we stop some of the blur and focus on the truly important details? Try making a list of two to four elements that are essential to include in your mission statement. These passions or values can help in writing a mission statement now and help focus the blur of life later.

It can be revised. Keep in mind that a mission statement can always be revised. Today's mission need not be next year's vision. My original mission statement was: "To love God, people, and ideas in balanced and healthy ways, and to help others do the same."

I wrote this at a time when I needed better balance in my life. But as our missions direct and energize us, we deal with problem areas and identify new challenges. Thus, my mission statement has changed, and no longer includes the concept of balance.

My current mission statement is: "To carefully explore ideas and show them to others while faithfully resting in God's love."

This mission statement is similar to the first—I see myself as a steward of ideas, energized by thinking and passing my thoughts to my children, my students, and those who read my writing. But also notice it has changed. I'm learning to rest more and worry less, so I include this idea in my mission statement. I'm paying close attention to faithfulness in my life, so I want to faithfully rest in God's love. I'm sure my mission statement will continue to change as my life progresses.

A mission statement casts a vision. Most of us remember pictures better than words. In fact, many of those with outstanding memories use pictures as tools to remember words. Ideally, a mission statement is more than a few words on a piece of paper—it creates a picture that is memorable and motivating.

With my mission statement, I picture myself as a child, sitting on the floor sorting through my projects and piles of ideas, while God is sitting behind me in a rocking chair reading a book. If anything happens to me, God will be there to help. If I have something to say, God will immediately put the book down and be available to listen. I am learning to rest in God's presence.

Different words will produce different pictures. The pictures go with us, reminding us of the things we value and energizing passions we hold.

Step 4: Keep It Available

Once written, a mission statement should be accessible so that it saturates one's way of thinking, feeling, and acting. When Moses wanted the Israelites to be transformed by God's laws, he instructed:

> Impress them on your children. Talk about them when you sit at home and when you walk along the road, when you lie down and when you get up. Tie them as symbols on your hands and bind them on your foreheads. Write them on the door frames of your houses and on your gates.

Moses knew what behavioral scientists know today: We must be repeatedly exposed to some things in order to learn them well.

Tying a mission statement on one's hands or binding them on one's forehead may take this principle a bit too far. But putting a mission statement on a refrigerator door or on the dashboard of the car may accomplish the same goal of letting one's vision saturate her or his lifestyle. A mission in life helps us move beyond ourselves and toward greater wisdom and purpose.

These first three principles for authenticity have been personal—they can be done alone. But as our mission is cast, it propels us into a world of people. Being true to our mission requires us to take risks with others, to pursue interpersonal relationships, and to think carefully about social authenticity—the focus of the next three chapters.

10

ESTABLISH AUTHENTIC RELATIONSHIPS

In order for us to be authentic with others, we must let others know us. In order for others to be authentic with us, we must know them. This hardly seems profound, but this obvious truth is sometimes masked by our intimacy-starved culture. Millions of Americans sink into an easy chair each night to watch the latest situation comedy or the newest video release because they lack alternatives. Many interact with people all day—at the lunch meeting, on the cellular phone, in the coffee room—but rarely achieve an intimate, trusting, authentic relationship.

As more and more authors write about addiction as disease, I wonder about expanding our ideas of disease. We label the sex addict, alcoholic, and drug addict "sick" and send them to hospitals and 12-step meetings. But maybe the sickness goes deeper than we know. Addiction may be a disease of a society whose members lack true intimacy. Those starving for emotional closeness often settle for counterfeit satisfaction—sex, excess food, alcohol, and so on.

An essential principle to becoming authentic people is allowing others to know us, including our emotions, struggles, and temptations. The problem is that some relationships have an appearance of intimacy, but they don't lead to greater authenticity. Truly authentic relationships need to be distinguished from other relationships.

When Relationships Don't Help

Throughout this book, I've suggested that confiding relationships help us manage our desires for pleasure and approval, but only if the relationships are healthy. Many relationships are involved without being intimate, confiding relationships. Consider some examples:

- Delores and Roseanne have been friends for years. They have coffee at one another's houses to keep up on the latest neighborhood news. They discuss politics, religion, their children's accomplishments, and community events. But neither risks to tell the other about her inner struggles, fears, or temptations. Neither risks vulnerability.

- Dana has not learned to understand love in her thirty-five years. She believes love and sex are identical. Even casual encounters with men end in her bedroom.

- Jon and George go to the bar together after work several nights a week. They sit at a table discussing their boss, commenting about women walking by, and encouraging one another to drink and dance more. They joke about going to hell so they can be with their friends.

- Mike and Linda are friends and coworkers. They feel they need their friendship to help cope with their lousy marriages. Both are looking for someone who will love them for who they are, unconditionally. They feel attracted to one another, and wish they would have met earlier in life.

- Trudy and Bill have known each other for several months, ever since Trudy confessed her struggles with an unforgiving attitude in church one morning. Bill, an elder, meets with Trudy to help her memorize Scripture. Trudy has started missing some of their weekly meetings. Bill is wondering if her excuses are legitimate.

All of these have the appearance of close relationships. But none of them help in the quest for authenticity, because these examples are relationships which come mostly from Jekyll and Hyde rather than a truth-focused desire for authenticity.

Jekyll meets Jekyll. Delores and Roseanne work carefully to keep their relationship safe. They prefer to discuss issues on the surface of their lives rather than exploring their deepest emotions and struggles. Both enjoy their relationship and look forward to having coffee together.

They have a fine relationship, the kind we all need to enjoy in life. Not every relationship needs to be intimate and confiding and those who are not able to enjoy surface relationships often drive others away with their intensity.

The primary force that maintains surface relationships is our Jekyll image. We don't want others to think badly of us, so we keep our conversations safe and shallow. The thoughts that keep relationships shallow are self-protective: "If I told Roseanne I disagree with her, she might not like me as much." "If Delores knew about my temper problem with the kids, she might not be my friend anymore." Again, this is not bad—glossy side desires help us function socially. Most people have many surface relationships in their lives. But these relationships will never meet our desires for intimacy and authenticity.

Hyde meets Hyde. Dana's relationships with men might be seen as intimate by some, just as Jon and George might believe the are looking for intimate relationships with women at the bar. But this type of intimacy comes from the dark side—intimacy driven by biological urges and attractions.

Dana made better choices with counseling, but why? It was not because of any great psychological insights or because she worked through repressed memories of abuse. It had nothing to do with her "inner child," her "codependence," or any of the other fads we read about these days. Dana improved because she was able to have a caring nonsexual relationship with a male for the first time. She began to authentically explore her own motives and values and conflicts because she found someone she could trust to treat her as a human being, not as a sexual object.

Some relationships, like Jon and George's, are built around the dark side urges of each person. With their words they joke about going to hell to be with their friends, but on a deeper level they justify their own pleasure-seeking urges by being with their equally impulsive friends.

This is more evidence of a sick society. Rather than struggling with temptations, many have decided to stop fighting and live according to Hyde's desires. Individualism, self-centeredness, and narcissism abound, and some dare to think of this as authenticity. But this type of authenticity is based on a naturalistic ethic that compares humans to rabbits or coyotes, and overlooks the human capacity to make sense of our biological urges and transcend our animal nature.

Mike and Linda's friendship seems wonderful to them—it helps them cope with their unhappy marriages. And each of them is looking for the same thing: to be loved unconditionally. It sounds reasonable, at least at first glance.

But they are caught in a narcissistic fantasy, drawing close to each other to gain warmth and security. They are dropping responsibilities to their spouses because the warmth they feel elsewhere is so powerful. They are headed for problems—problems caused when dark side desires are confused with authentic relationships.

Relationships based on dark-side urges may carry a myth of authenticity, but the driving force behind them comes from our animal nature—our desire to have pleasure. These desires are not all bad, but they form a poor foundation for authentic relationships.

Jekyll meets Hyde. Some relationships cannot reach a level of deep trust and authenticity because the relationship is based on one person "fixing" another. Bill meets with Trudy each week to help her with unforgiveness. He has her memorize Bible passages and tells her the evils of anger. Is this an authentic relationship? Probably not.

Bill's Jekyll is in a relationship with Trudy's Hyde. Their relationship has no symmetry or flexibility. Imagine the following conversation:

> TRUDY: I've been thinking about what you've been saying and I'm not sure I agree. I think it's normal to be angry and I don't think I can forgive someone until I'm honest about my anger.
>
> BILL: Remember, Satan is the master of disguise. If you open the door to anger, it will take over your life.
>
> TRUDY: I suppose you're right.

This example shows a rigid style of relating where Trudy is the irresponsible child and Bill is the wise adult. Unfortunately, once the roles are established, Bill and Trudy will find it difficult to relate in more balanced ways. Trudy is probably right that anger is normal, but the rules of the relationship overrule the validity of her point. In authentic relationships, one person does not try to fix the other.

• •

SELF-AWARENESS EXERCISE:

Take several minutes to list relationships in your life that have not worked out well. In each case, see if the relationship was based on a false concept of authenticity.

Jekyll meets Jekyll: A relationship that remained shallow because of a desire to look good or avoid risk.

Hyde meets Hyde: A relationship that felt good for a while but lacked responsibility and sensibility.

Jekyll meets Hyde: A relationship where one person was trying to fix the other.

If it is still possible to improve the relationship, what ideas might help you and the other person change the nature of the relationship?

• •

Relationships That Help

Some relationships, unlike the ones highlighted so far in this chapter, bring us to greater maturity and wisdom. These are often long-lasting relationships that change the fabric of our lives.

I now know what I didn't know before buying a sofa and love seat several years ago. Lisa and I liked the look of the white furniture and paid extra to have a fabric protection applied. However, our kids, their friends, and dirty hands and feet outlasted the fabric protection. We have since been told about two different products. One is a surface coat that goes on the outside of the fabric. It protects the furniture for a while, but eventually wears off. The other penetrates the fibers of the material and lasts as long as the furniture. Unfortunately, we had the first type of fabric protection.

A similar distinction can be made with friendship. Some friends stick on the surface of our lives, and we enjoy and help one another for a while. But other friendships change our very nature by saturating the fabric of life and compelling us to be bolder and better than we were before.

These soul-mate friendships bring smiles to our faces as our memories span the gap of time or miles that remove us from the other. They bring energy and make us more compassionate and honest to others and ourselves. Though not an expert, I have observed and experienced enough to recognize some distinguishing characteristics of this type of friendship.

Nondemanding acceptance. Intimate friends have a supporting acceptance of one another that allows each to prosper. They are able to balance their delight in being together with a desire for each to develop independently as a person. They are neither completely dependent on one another nor completely independent of one another. They are interdependent and flexible: dependent on each other in times of need, independent of each other when days or weeks go by with little contact but with the knowledge that the other still cares, and a good team when they are together.

A proverb tells us, "There are but two bequests we give our children: One is roots, the other is wings." The same two gifts abound in intimate friendship with nondemanding acceptance. Being nondemanding requires giving the other wings, encouraging growth and giving support, wanting the best for the friend even when it is personally inconvenient or painful. When Lisa and I decided to move our family across the country in the middle of our lives, my friend Clark was saddened but excited for the new opportunities that faced me. I remember the day he told me that he felt excited for me and thought I would fit in well where I was going. Perhaps without knowing, he blessed my decision—the same decision he had grieved several weeks before. He gave me wings.

The roots of friendship are found in acceptance. With acceptance comes a form of commitment that says:

"I will care for you regardless of what happens."

"I may not approve of everything you do, but I will remain your friend."

These roots shatter glossy side urges and free people to be authentic and honest with themselves and their friends.

Understanding the other's mission. Intimate friends understand and help shape the other's mission. This is part of seeing ourselves through the eyes of another.

Several years ago, in a small Oregon town, two families developed a friendship. They began meeting together on a weekly basis to support and encourage one another. As they learned about each other, they began to plan together, to support as a group the mission of individual members. As a result, the community has been changed. Their town now has a private Christian school with modest tuition, small class sizes, and a good working relationship with the public schools. There is a fitness program for those at risk for heart disease. And there is a growing congregation of several hundred people who meet weekly for a nontraditional time of worship. These things happened because individual missions were supported by intimate friends.

Even the Lone Ranger wasn't alone, but had Tonto to support his endeavors. Friends help each other define and accomplish their missions in life.

Tolerance for the truth. Intimate friends tolerate the truth from one another, even truths they can't tolerate from someone else. This involves speaking the truth and hearing the truth. Both require personal risk. Imagine the following situation:

> Pat and Mike are nondemanding, supportive friends who are beginning to trust one another with the authentic details of their lives. Before they meet for breakfast one morning, Pat has an argument with his wife, Jill, who has been lying awake for several hours stewing about how Pat criticizes her in public. Pat thinks she is just feeling sorry for herself and tells her to go back to sleep. They end up yelling at each other before Pat stomps out the door, slamming it as he leaves.

Speaking the truth requires overcoming the fear of rejection. If Pat tells Mike what happened before their breakfast meeting, he risks shattering Mike's image of him as a supportive and caring husband. But let's assume Pat overcomes these fears and tells Mike. Pat speaks the truth.

Mike listens and replies, "That sounds like a tense morning, Pat!" Pat feels affirmed and understood. Mike has not overstepped his invitation and has been an accepting listener. The conversation goes well and trust is deepened.

Now what if the same thing happens three weeks later and Pat takes an additional risk at their next meeting: "Mike, Jill keeps telling me I put her down in public. Have you ever noticed me doing that?" Assuming Mike has noticed some social "put-downs," what is he to do in response to this question? The caring, though risky, response is to answer honestly: "Pat, I have noticed that on occasion."

In the first case, Mike did not offer his opinion because it was not invited. Uninvited opinions come across as easy answers and are usually not well-received. In the second, his opinion was invited and he honestly replied. In the best friendships, like the one Pat and Mike are developing, people can tolerate honesty. Both honestly reveal themselves, and both respond kindly and frankly to the other.

Perhaps the most ideal and natural place for authentic friendship is in marriage. Unfortunately, many are unable to attain a marriage of this stature, even those who are mature and committed to one another. But when friendship and marriage coincide, home becomes a sanctuary.

Psychologist Abraham Maslow found that healthy people are less defensive and more vulnerable in their love relationships. Maslow summarized what an authentic relationship looks like: "They can feel psychologically naked and still feel loved and wanted and secure."

Authenticity begins with self-understanding, but cannot be complete until it involves caring, confiding relationships. Both are essential. Intimate relationships allow the separateness of two lives within the community of one friendship. In *The Prophet*, Kahlil Gibran writes: "And stand together yet not too near together; For the pillars of the temple stand apart, and the oak tree and the cypress grow not in each other's shadow." We stand far enough apart for self-understanding, and close enough together for honesty and love.

11

BECOME A VULNERABLE HELPER

Whoever told us "talk is cheap" was obviously speaking before the day of psychotherapy and 900 numbers. But there is some truth in the saying, and other clichés support the same idea:

"Put your money where your mouth is."

"It's easier said than done."

All of these converge on the idea of backing up our speech with actions. Authentic people are not content to talk about helping others; they become vulnerable helpers—vulnerable because they are willing to sacrifice their own comfort to help someone else.

Jesus told a parable about a Jewish man walking down the 17 miles of steep road between Jerusalem and Jericho, a country dwelling of priests. On the way, he was ambushed by thieves who robbed him, took his clothes, wounded him, and then left him to die. He needed help. The first two who passed by him were religious leaders, undoubtedly respected for their piety and character. But they didn't stop to help. The third, a member of an ethnic minority group despised by many Jews, stopped and bandaged the man's wounds, then took him to an inn and paid for his lodging and care. This simple story has been told and retold countless times in the past two millennia because it contains the same truth as those clichés. It's not enough to talk the talk: Authenticity requires us to put our beliefs into action.

Each of the characters in the story of the Good Samaritan is an archetype of people in every culture and every time. Two characters in the story reflect the authenticity we strive for. We can learn from those characters, and also from the others.

Your Stuff Should Be Mine

The first characters the man came across were thieves. Their philosophy was, "Your stuff should be mine." They were ruled by their dark sides, and were after immediate gratification. No story is complete without an evil, selfish character. In the story of the Good Samaritan, the robbers represent this role.

Authenticity requires personal ethical standards, because exploitation can occur almost secretly. Our family recently discussed personal ethics on the way to a pizza restaurant. We found two coupons for five free game tokens, but only one coupon could be used per purchase. We discussed the option of getting ten free tokens by splitting our order in two: Lisa could order the pizza and I could order breadsticks and soft drinks. Although we weren't sure that this "divide and conquer" mentality was unethical, we ultimately decided it went against the intent of the coupon and settled for five free tokens.

Life is full of opportunities to exploit others, and exploitation is easy to justify by convincing ourselves we deserve what we want. But authenticity requires us to rise above the "getting mentality" that motivated the robbers on that winding road from Jerusalem to Jericho.

Ignorance Is Bliss

More subtle than the aggression of the robbers is the apathy of the religious leaders who walked by the wounded man without stopping to help. Ignoring those in pain hinders us from authentic encounters with others who need our compassion and help. Why do we ignore them?

First, we ignore others because we feel too busy to stop and help. Perhaps the men were on their way to an important meeting. Maybe they were on their way to help someone else in need. When they were confronted with a more immediate need, they justified walking on because they were too busy. The story helps put the busyness in perspective. We conclude, how could anyone be too busy to stop and help someone in such a crisis? Yet crises are all around us.

A second reason we ignore those in pain comes from our glossy side desire to have all the answers. While one is driving an expensive car and talking on a cellular phone, another is digging through trash cans for scraps to eat. The one in the car reasons, "If bums had as much initiative as I, they would be eating filet mignon instead of sandwich crusts." The religious leaders may have had similar thoughts. "If he lies there long enough, he'll regain his strength and be fine." By denying problems, we shield ourselves from the pathos of those around us.

A third reason is the just-world assumption. Psychologists have demonstrated that we assume those in pain deserve to be in pain. This is even true when a victim is selected at random. In one study, for example, college students watched as a peer was chosen at random and then given electric shocks for missing items on a memory test (actually, the shocks were staged and the victim was a confederate in the experiment). When asked about the shocks, the observers concluded the victim deserved to be shocked for being "so dumb." The religious leaders may have assumed that the victim was lying in the ditch because God was judging him for disobedience. Thus, they felt less obligation to help. The executive in the car sees the homeless person searching for food and concludes, "Bums get what they deserve for being lazy."

Taken together, these reasons for ignoring others' pain suggest we are often too self-focused to help. We're too busy, too trite in our views, too quick to assume justice where it doesn't exist. As the Good Samaritan story portrays, even "good" people are prone to ignoring those in pain.

Being a Helper

These first characters in our story are not good role models for authenticity. But along comes a man from Samaria, one of the hated half-breeds, who sees another human in need, looks beyond ethnic differences, and becomes a vulnerable helper. The Samaritan had a choice—he could remain safely uninvolved, or he could risk his own comfort, becoming vulnerable to help another in need. At the end of the story, Jesus asked which character had loved his neighbor. In this context, we might ask which character was the most genuine. In either case, the answer is seen in the title—the Good Samaritan.

Vulnerable helpers, like the Good Samaritan, have several distinguishing characteristics.

They understand pain. Vulnerable helpers experience empathy. They weep with those who weep, and rejoice with those who rejoice.

Though we have hundreds of graduate training programs for counselors in the United States, I'm convinced the best counselors have an ability to empathize that cannot be learned in the classroom. It is an interpersonal skill they have learned throughout life. They can sense pain in others and are perceived as concerned and caring people.

Empathy requires that we avoid easy answers. It forces us into the life of the other person where we can better understand his or her situation and feelings. In the biblical account of Job, several of his friends came to support him after he lost his family and fortune. Although they later resorted to uninvited opinions, they started with empathy. They came and sat for seven days and seven nights without saying a word. They understood Job's pain.

Denying the pain others feel is an obvious obstacle to empathy. By closing our eyes to the pain of others, we protect ourselves from discomfort. If the Good Samaritan had reasoned, "I've never experienced this kind of pain, so that fellow over there must not be in pain," we would see it as ridiculous logic. But how often do we do the same with world hunger, people dying of AIDS, those without adequate medical care, and so on? Denial of pain is a self-focused strategy that interferes with authenticity.

Perhaps some deny pain because they see it as all bad. Actually, there is value in pain. Pain is not intrinsically good, but it can cause good. Psychologist Lawrence Al Siebert, who has studied those surviving great emotional and physical pain, concluded in a newspaper interview: "A typical expression of a person with a survival personality is, 'I would never willingly go through anything like that again, but it was probably the best thing that could ever have happened to me.'" The survivor sees value in suffering.

In facing pain, we learn more about the nature of life. In the widely-quoted opening paragraph of *The Road Less Traveled*, M. Scott

Peck writes that life is difficult and, paradoxically, once we learn to accept life as difficult, it is no longer difficult. Accepting pain changes our worldview and life no longer seems as painful. Pain often causes growth.

They are motivated by pain. The wounded man's pain motivated the Good Samaritan to help him. Authenticity often requires us to act in response to the pain we see.

In one sense, pain motivates us all. A pounding headache gets us looking for the Advil. We make a dental appointment promptly once a tooth starts hurting. A sore knee makes us give up exercising for a while. We are biologically motivated by pain.

But the Good Samaritan was motivated by the pain of another. There was no promise of getting anything in return. He helped because he saw someone in pain, and he cared.

Most of the noble actions in the world go unnoticed because they are not performed by the rich and famous, but by the everyday people who are motivated by pain: the ones who spend weekend evenings handing out sandwiches to the homeless, the one who watches her neighbor's children so the neighbor can visit her father in the hospital, the one who prepares a meal for a family in crisis, the one who works overtime so a coworker can visit a dying relative. Being motivated by the pain of another allows us to be vulnerable helpers.

They give hope. The Good Samaritan gave hope to a suffering man. Hope makes pain bearable.

On a hot August day my old Plymouth Duster began to spew forth steam from its clogged radiator. After pulling to the side of the road and evaluating the situation, I realized the radiator was nearly empty. Ten miles from the nearest city and nine hundred miles from my college destination, a cloud of despair settled over me as I planned my next action. The vast nothingness of I-5 was shattered only by an occasional vehicle speeding by. As I began to plan my hitchhike to the nearest town, a man in a pickup truck pulled off the freeway and offered assistance. Not only was he willing to help me, he had a 200-gallon drum of water in the back of his pickup. After cooling off the engine, he filled my radiator with water, allowing me to make it to the next town for repairs. Like the good Samaritan, he gave a gift of hope: I could make it.

There are two types of hope: one that is self-focused and shallow and another that infuses meaning into life regardless of circumstances. In one sense, being rescued on my college trip gave a self-focused hope—I knew I could get to the next town for necessary repairs. But there was a deeper lesson in that experience. I remember feeling shocked that a stranger would stop and help me for no apparent reason. That experience deepened my hope in human goodness. The man who was robbed along that Jerusalem road was given immediate hope—he lived through the crisis. But I suspect he was also given a deeper hope, a hope that revolutionized the way he viewed and treated Samaritans. Authentic helpers point others to deep hope that abounds in the midst of trials and struggles.

Superficial hope focuses on self, it looks only for escape from struggles. This deeper hope focuses on truth, allowing us to look beyond self-centered needs and find peace in the midst of turmoil.

Helping and Hoping

There are four common ways of finding hope in the midst of pain. The first three work well in some situations, but not with long-standing pain.

The first option is to avoid pain. Superficial hope seeks solutions. It is reasonable and good to avoid pain when possible, but sometimes pain is unavoidable.

It's like an end sweep in football. To avoid defenders, halfbacks run to the edge of the field and then attempt to turn upfield. Sometimes they successfully avoid the defense and are able to gain many yards on the play. Other times, they run toward the sidelines, but the defense runs with them and they are tackled without gain. Similarly, sometimes our efforts to avoid pain are successful and other times they are not.

The second option is to deny pain in order to feel hope. Denial is a useful psychological defense, but eventually it obscures truth and causes problems. By "hocus pocus" we sometimes think we can remove pain.

One man described a traumatic incident after his eighteen-year-old son died in a drowning accident. As he left the funeral home where he was making preparations for the memorial service, a well-meaning Christian walked up and asked if he was the one who just lost his son. When the grieving father answered affirmatively, the other man smiled, patted him on the shoulder and said, "Praise the Lord!" Saying "Praise the Lord!" to someone who has just lost his son is insensitive. Pain is not so easily removed.

The third option is to see hope as relief, the thank-God-it's-Friday mentality. This relief-seeking hope causes football players to count the days until "daily doubles" are over, or students to number the days of class left before summer break. It is the hope I begin to have on the ninth hole of the golf course, recognizing my misery will soon be over. But relief doesn't always come in life. Sometimes pain continues relentlessly. Seeking relief is fine, but not always realistic.

Transcendent hope is the fourth option. Sometimes life's pain forces us to look deeper for hope than we otherwise would. Cellular telephones, job promotions, new-release movies, and pension accounts suddenly have less value. The things we used to put our hope in don't mean much anymore. Then out of the debris of life emerges a hope that is richer and more mature than that experienced before—a hope that transcends the trivial circumstances that consume most of our time and allows us to find a deeper meaning in life. It's a hope that many describe to be inseparable from faith.

Psychologist Victor Frankl was imprisoned in a concentration camp during World War II. He worked each day to find hope— reconstructing a manuscript on scraps of paper, visualizing being reunited with his wife, believing that there must be some greater meaning to life than what he had previously known. He believed he would endure the hardships and survive the terror. He found hope in the midst of pain. This deepest level of hope prepares us for greater levels of authenticity as we learn to value the things that are most important and put in perspective the trivia that normally captures our attention. Transcendent hope moves us from being self-focused to being truth-focused.

The Good Samaritan brought hope to a suffering man. In one sense it was superficial hope: bandages for wounds, a warm place to spend the night, food to nourish his body. But in another sense it was a transcendent hope that pointed to human goodness, altruism, and the victory of love over ethnic differences.

Authentic Encounters

Being a vulnerable helper requires authentic interactions with others. The religious leaders passed by a suffering man, perhaps on their way to deliver a sermon or offer a sacrifice to God. Their encounters with others were tainted with their choice to ignore another's pain. The most authentic encounter that day was between two people who might have been enemies under different circumstances. And it only occurred because the Samaritan empathized with pain and gave hope to a suffering man.

••

SELF-AWARENESS EXERCISE:

Think carefully over the past 24 hours. Who have you encountered that is experiencing pain? Think of a practical way you might empathize with that pain (e.g. a card, a telephone call, words of understanding). Are there practical actions that would help ease the pain and bring an awareness of greater hope?

••

Authenticity requires us to pay a price. Sometimes it means putting cash in an envelope and sending it anonymously to someone in need who wouldn't accept it if they knew who sent it. Sometimes it requires us to be late to an appointment. Sometimes authentic helping means we cry with or hold the hand of someone in pain. It means praying to God on behalf of others because we told them we would.

The world is filled with great leaders. They speak from pulpits, give lectures, write books, and make audio and video tapes. Many are authentic leaders who disclose their personal struggles and empathize with the pain of their audience. We need authentic leaders. But even more, we need vulnerable helpers. We need those who sense another's pain, set aside their own goals, and give help and hope. These authentic encounters happen one-on-one in inconspicuous places, like on that road between Jerusalem and Jericho. And they make the difference.

12

SPEAK HONESTLY WITH HUMILITY

With my knees knocking and my voice quivering, I stood before my high school class delivering a graduation speech. The point of my four-minute talk was that we need one another, that interdependence was better than independence. The speech was mostly memorized since I had already delivered it many times to the unresponsive mirror. As I look back on those four adrenaline-filled minutes, I realize a strange irony of public speaking. Though I had carefully selected my words and practiced a cogent delivery, I cared less about what I had to say than about what people thought of me.

This is not all bad. Those glossy side desires to appear competent compelled me to prepare carefully, inject interesting illustrations, and support my assertions with evidence. Probably most public speakers care about their listeners' impressions. But when impressing others causes the truth to be altered or suppressed, authenticity is smothered and people get hurt.

Whether we're standing in front of a group of high school graduates, chatting with friends in the living room, or discussing politics with coworkers in the break room, we all have opportunities to speak in front of others, and these are opportunities for public authenticity. When we present ourselves to others, two things are important as we strive to become more authentic people: honesty and humility.

Honesty

Imagine the following situation: As you sit on stage waiting for the program to begin, you watch people streaming in the entrances to fill the large arena. The months of advertising your speech have obviously worked—thousands have come. They come to hear you, an expert on parenting. Stacks of audio speakers sit on each side of the stage as technicians busily check sound levels and lighting conditions. After a flattering introduction, you rise from your chair amidst the applause and walk to the podium. You open your mouth and begin your speech.

Think for a moment about what you would tell this hungry audience about parenting. What advice would you give? What stories would you tell? Most of us would tell of our success experiences. I would recount the time my one-year-old daughter wanted to walk to the moon. Rather than discouraging her blind ambition, I decided to let her discover the world for herself. So I said, "All right, let's walk to the moon." We took off, hand-in-hand across our yard, into the vacant field next door. The grass was tall and Danielle asked me to carry her. "No," I replied, "if we're going to walk to the moon we each should walk on our own." After several minutes Danielle concluded it was just too far to walk to the moon, so we turned around and went home.

That story has taken on mythical greatness in our household because it speaks of a patient father spending time to let his daughter discover something new about the world. I would be inclined to tell that story.

But let's go back to our imaginary situation. Let's add one other detail: As you walk to the podium, you gaze into the stands where your eager audience sits. You organize your notes, look up to say your first words, and notice to your surprise that your entire family is sitting in the front row. You didn't know they were coming! They want to hear what you have to say about parenting.

At this point, most of us would have a problem. If Danielle were sitting in the front row, she would hear my success story about our moon walk, but she sees the bigger picture. Danielle was in the car the time we got stuck in a snow storm and the chains came off one of the tires. She heard me shouting and stomping around like an idiot.

She knows about the times I lose my patience, make unreasonable demands, and don't listen attentively. Danielle knows I am not the perfect father.

Most of us don't make speeches to large groups of people, but let's go back to the example of chatting with friends in the living room. In the course of the conversation, imagine the topic of parenting comes up. What will you say about parenting? Will you say anything different about your parenting successes and failures if your children are sitting in the living room? If they are playing Nintendo downstairs?

All of us are public speakers—sometimes in large groups, sometimes in small groups. Authentic public speaking means we say the same things whether or not those close to us are listening, and that the things we say are honest. Those who live one life in public and another in private leave permanent scars on family and friends—I have seen it dozens of times in the counseling office.

Honesty requires personal vulnerability. A high price of honesty is taking risks in the presence of others. Putting one's best foot forward may impress those who listen, but honesty gets lost in the process.

It is not wrong to make a positive impression when speaking to others, but when making that impression obscures a truthful, honest presentation, the speaker's priorities deserve a careful look. Perhaps this is why politicians are the subject of so much suspicion. Several highly publicized cases have exposed the falsehoods of our national leaders. Not all politicians fit this mold, but the visible cases of fraud and deception have made most of us wary and suspicious.

The same tragedy sometimes happens in our local churches and community organizations. Some in leadership roles are well-meaning men and women who sometimes resort to making a good impression when the truth doesn't sound good enough. What results? In many cases, people become suspicious, avoid the organization, and speak critically of it to their friends: "Don't go to that church; it's filled with hypocrites!"

Is the church really filled with hypocrites? Probably not. It's just a group of people like you and me who want to be liked by others. Sometimes we cover a bit of the truth or sound optimistic about our faith to make a good impression. Honesty gets compromised in the process, and people walk out the sanctuary doors committed to staying away forever.

Honesty comes with risk. If I disclose to you my real struggles, then you might reject me and that is risky. But trying to look good by avoiding honest disclosure has its own risks. If I never tell you my struggles, over time you will realize my self-protective strategy and may withdraw from me. Either option has risks. Once the risk is confronted, only honesty allows for greater insight and intimacy.

Honesty encourages others to be honest. Vulnerable honesty gives others hope and escape from the loneliness of their personal struggles. It is comforting to be reminded that others walk beside us in the midst of life's good times and bad times.

Let's enter into the middle of a conversation between two couples:

> CANDY: My work has been so demanding lately. I'm just hoping it gets better when the Christmas season ends.
> DON: I figure work is important, but I'm not going to let it run my life. My family has to come first.

Lois, Don's wife, knows better. Don puts in twelve-hour days, makes business calls from home, and sends his kids to the other room when they interrupt. Lois recognizes Don's glossy side when she sees it! Very likely she will respond to his glibness with resentment.

Now let's rewind the conversation and see how Don could have responded.

> CANDY: My work has been so demanding lately. I'm just hoping it gets better when the Christmas season ends.
> DON: That's a real challenge for me too, Candy. I work too many hours and find it really hard to cut back.
> CANDY: Why does this happen? You get a job you really like, and soon it starts taking over your life.
> LOIS: And it really affects family life too.
> ED: That's for sure.

This conversation is more honest than the last version, and it is mutually supportive. Both couples now feel free to discuss the problems of job stress and family demands.

When our friends had their lives unravel several years ago because the husband's substance addiction was discovered, they were publicly embarrassed and personally devastated. Since the dust has settled, dozens of others have come to them to discuss personal problems, addictions, and temptations. Our friends have become vulnerable helpers to many.

Authenticity is beautiful because it allows us to honestly explore our struggles together, sharing our burdens with one another. We gain wisdom and encouragement as we navigate life with others. Authenticity is a team sport.

Honesty does not require total disclosure. It would be a mistake to imply that honesty requires us to disclose everything about ourselves. Total disclosure almost guarantees driving others away, and it often isn't as authentic as it appears.

Let's imagine Henry and Frank conversing about politics. Henry considers himself progressive and Frank sees himself as a conservative. They see the problem of homelessness very differently. Here's the conversation:

> HENRY: I'm deeply concerned about the number of homeless people in urban America. Something needs to be done.
>
> FRANK: Yes, something does need to be done, but I think the responsibility is on the homeless, not on us. Most of them could work if they took the initiative.
>
> HENRY: Do you really think so? It seems to me that many of the homeless have mental illnesses and substance abuse problems that keep them from getting regular jobs.
>
> FRANK: I suppose so, but some of those problems would get better if they took more responsibility.

So far, Frank and Henry have politely disagreed, each honestly stating his opinion without attacking the other. But what if either of them confuses honesty with total disclosure? Imagine what might happen.

> HENRY: I get so tired of you rednecks! You reduce things down to simple views that aren't true in the real world. My dad used to do the same stuff. I think you're pretty stupid to see it that way.

> FRANK: You liberals are so arrogant! You assume all the world's problems can be solved with some new government program or higher taxes. Well, I'm tired of paying for your lame ideas and wish you guys would just shut up.

It's possible that these statements accurately reflect what Henry and Frank are feeling during their conversation, but expressing these feelings would only drive a wedge between them and make it more difficult to communicate in the future.

It is unwise to disclose all the personal struggles we face to one another, especially to those who are only casual acquaintances. Many things can backfire when we give more information than another is ready to hear:

- The person might give a recipe-like answer for how to solve the problem.
- The person might embellish the story and tell it to someone else.
- The person might be scared or threatened by your personal disclosure and avoid you in the future.
- You might be embarrassed about what you said and avoid the person in the future.
- Your disclosure might create bruised feelings, confusion, or uncertainty for the other person.

We can be honest without telling every detail about ourselves.

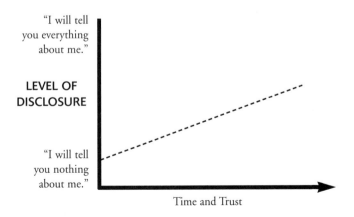

Appropriate disclosure increases with time and trust, as this graph shows. On the first meeting, two people reveal relatively little about themselves, even though they may be completely honest. After they become friends, they reveal more. With time, trust builds and self-disclosure increases. But even in the most intimate human relationship, marriage, we don't disclose 100 percent of ourselves to the other, though the marriage may be filled with honesty and openness.

••

SELF-AWARENESS EXERCISE:

Try a self-disclosure experiment. Think of one thing about yourself that you don't like. Choose something that's not too personal. Now think of one person you could tell your fault to, along with a specific goal for change. Call the person or meet for coffee and describe your fault. Observe how the person responds.

••

I tried this recently to correct a fault. I had been whining about bad calls while playing noon basketball with my friends. It's not much fun when someone gets too competitive, and that's what I had been doing. So I chose a friend in the locker room before the next game and told him I was embarrassed about my whining and wanted to stop. If I whined again, I would voluntarily not play the following day. Telling him my fault helped me keep my competitive impulses under control and after the game he smiled and said, "I guess you can play tomorrow." It was an affirming experience where honesty added to friendship and helped me correct a fault.

Humility

The apostle Paul instructed his readers to "Let your conversation be always full of grace, seasoned with salt." His advice is wise. If honesty is the salt in our speech, our general attitude needs to be saturated with humility. There are several reasons for this.

Life unfolds gradually. The things that seem clear today may seem more complicated in the future. Idealism erodes with experience and words of the past come back to haunt us.

Remember the imaginary situation at the beginning of this chapter. Eager eyes watch as you deliver a speech on parenting. Let's imagine you have developed an effective technique for parenting preschoolers and you describe your technique with confidence, asserting that it works for children of any age. The crowd leaves motivated to try your parenting method. But when your children grow, you discover it doesn't work so well for teenagers. Oops. The words of the past came from good intentions, but also from inadequate experience. Now they haunt you. We need humility because we always have more to learn.

We overestimate ourselves. A second reason to be humble is that scientific studies repeatedly demonstrate that we overestimate the validity our opinions. To exaggerate slightly, "I said it, I believe it, and that's good enough for me."

If test subjects are randomly assigned to argue two different sides of an issue, they begin to believe whatever side they argue. Psychologist David Myers concludes, "Saying is believing." And once an opinion is formed, it is very hard to change because humans look for evidence that confirms their beliefs and avoid evidence that refutes their beliefs.

When I teach general psychology, I have eight students stand in front of the class and tell a story from their past. The story can be either true or false. Then I have the remaining students guess whether it is a true story or a false story, and how sure they are that their guess is correct. The students are notoriously poor at guessing the correct answer, but extremely confident that they are correct. This overconfidence phenomenon affects us all and requires us to be humble when we give our opinions and perspectives.

We have faults we don't see. A third reason to be humble is that others sometimes see us more accurately than we see ourselves. Our defense mechanisms keep us from seeing some of our most glaring characteristics and faults. Like the Emperor in his new clothes, we sometimes strut confidently in our supposed wisdom while others see the naked truth.

Ironically, our faults and our strengths are often the same characteristics. The strong, dynamic leader may be hard to be married to while being a tremendous corporate executive or military officer. The competitive person may not be fun to play Monopoly with, but may be self-disciplined and consistent. The careful analyzer can save a troubled institution from financial disaster, but be boring at home. The idealist organizes great activities and casts vision for the future, but is hard to live with when things don't go as planned.

These faults, the ones we can't see, cloud our vision and make our judgments suspect. We need humility to recognize our vulnerability to err.

Others will respond better. One person's authenticity helps another be authentic. If I honestly express myself to you, you will be more inclined to honestly express yourself to me or someone else. Authenticity is contagious, especially when honesty is tempered with humility.

Honesty without humility often has the opposite result. Imagine an acquaintance gives you this advice, and notice how you respond emotionally:

> I used to have a problem getting too angry at my family, but I figured out what to do. Now I close my eyes and imagine myself acting like a raving maniac and realize how ridiculous I look. Then I open my eyes and I don't feel angry at all. It works! Try it!

Though this may be honest for one person, most will not respond with greater authenticity. Why is this? Because many of us with families don't find it so easy to eliminate anger. And we might even question this person's experience. How many times has this technique worked? How angry was this person and would it work with different levels of anger?

When honesty is spoken without humility, others feel suspicious or cautious. But when honesty and humility go together, the response is different. What if the person said something like this:

> I've had a problem getting too angry at my family, but I am trying a new idea that seems to be helping. Now I close my eyes and imagine myself acting like a raving maniac and realize how ridiculous I look. Then I open my eyes and I seem to be able to manage my anger better. It probably won't work for everyone under every circumstance, but it is helping me.

This time the honesty is balanced with humility and most will respond with feelings of understanding and kindness. Such authenticity brings out the best in people.

Contemporary culture is so filled with messages of persuasion and public relations, it's hard to imagine a culture built on honesty and humility. Political speeches would be very different: "It's not likely that I can balance the budget, and taxes will probably increase. I have more experience with domestic policy than with foreign matters, but I'll do the best I can and surround myself with good advisers. I would appreciate your vote."

Advertisements would be different too. "This makeup costs more than other brands, but we think it's better and hope you'll buy it anyway." "Our after-shave doesn't really make you more attractive, but it feels good on your face." "We're planning to redesign this model next year, but we hope you'll buy one of our cars today."

These kinds of changes seem unlikely—it's doubtful that our culture will be based on honesty and humility anytime soon. But those brave enough to fight the tides of culture will find that honesty and humility move them toward greater authenticity.

So far we have discussed three principles of personal authenticity and three principles of social authenticity. The remaining principle is perhaps the most important and helps put the purpose of authenticity in its proper context.

13

ACCEPT GRACE

Although this book has included some self-help strategies, some basic problems can never be solved by focusing on them more intently. Some problems require self-analysis and personal concentration to solve, but others require us to look beyond the problem and find strength in someone greater than ourselves.

For millennia humans have looked for explanations and spiritual meaning in life's trials. Looking to and for God allows us to transcend our struggles and hidden addictions. The popularity and reported success of the 12-step recovery programs show the power of looking beyond ourselves to a transcendent Being who is available to help us and free us from our struggles with Jekyll and Hyde.

People often reject spiritual perspectives, sometimes with good reasons. After all, humans create religions to understand a God who can never be fully understood. Unfortunately, when people reject religion, they sometimes reject God also, and are left with only a shallow view of grace.

Grace is the active ingredient of the Christian faith. Christians believe they deserve punishment from God, but instead God grants them the gift of life. But many of us, even as Christians, misunderstand grace. We try to earn love in unhealthy ways: impressive accomplishment, unanimous approval, or demanding control. A healthy view of grace requires us to give up trying to *earn* love, and instead to *respond* to love. It gets our eyes off ourselves and onto someone else.

Grace makes love unconditional, pain bearable, and hope powerful. The road from self-focus to truth-focus is paved with grace. We all need grace to get beyond our natural ways of thinking and our self-defense mechanisms.

If-Then Mentality

Remember "if-then" statements from school mathematics and logic courses? The transitive property of mathematics is an example:

> If A is greater than B and B is greater than C, then A is greater than C.

We apply the same if-then thinking to numerous life experiences and social situations:

> If it rains on Tuesday, then we will not have the baseball game.

> If Patty does not act friendly, then I will know she is holding a grudge.

> If I do not study, then I will not pass the test.

If-then statements are logical. They seem natural to us, perhaps because most economic and social systems are based on exchange. If I give you thirty dollars, then you'll give me a pair of shoes. Social psychologists demonstrate a similar social phenomenon. If someone likes us, we'll probably like them. If someone gives us help, we'll help them in return.

Grace requires us to imagine "if-less thens," benevolent responses to unworthiness.

> "I love you regardless of what you do to me."

> "I will help you even if you can't pay for my time."

> "I will care about you no matter how evil your life has been."

These statements of grace transcend an if-then mentality.

Religion can be perceived either as an if-then arrangement or as an "if-less then." Some people see God as a predictable, even controllable, force who gives good gifts if humans act a certain way.

> "If I give ten percent of my money to the church, then God will make me rich."

> "If I faithfully pray and read the Bible then God will remove pain and health problems from my life."

This sort of "bad religion" can be found in homes and church buildings throughout the world, but so can a healthier form of religion—one that frees people to see God as gracious, though not predictable. Rather than trying to control God, those with healthy religious beliefs work to give up control—to yield to God's will and power. As they give up their efforts to control, they find peace and joy even in the midst of painful circumstances. The 12-step movement, which has helped millions of people live in victory over addictions, is based on this very paradox: Giving up control to God is the first step toward healing.

Grace and Self-focus

Grace and self-focus are incompatible. Those obsessed with themselves can never know grace, because grace requires us to see beyond ourselves. Grace can never be understood with an "if-then" mentality. The self-focused coping strategies—yielding to Jekyll and yielding to Hyde—miss the essence of grace.

Yielding to Jekyll. The glossy side of the personality demands perfection. Somewhere in childhood we convince ourselves that if our teeth are straight and white, our complexion clear, our clothes clean, and our attitude cheerful, then others will like us. Perhaps we are partly right—dozens of research studies show that attractive people are liked more than the unattractive.

But high school cheerleaders and athletes grow up, get wrinkles, lose hair, and gain weight. Then what? If acceptability comes only from appearing perfect, most of us are doomed to a life of loneliness.

Grace provides an alternative by suggesting we can be loved by God and others, even though we aren't perfect. On a logical level, this is a statement of the obvious—of course we can be loved in spite of our faults. But on a deep emotional level, many fail to recognize this simple truth.

Laura came for help because she was depressed and angry, ready to climb into her Toyota and drive away from her life. Maybe she would stop in New Mexico, or Texas, or Alabama—she didn't care, she just wanted out. As we discussed her situation, she revealed herself to be an expert at yielding to Jekyll. She hid her true feelings and passions, trying to be perfect so others would love her. But those around her didn't always show love, so she felt hurt and angry. She wanted to escape.

As we talked about her religious faith, Laura described feeling all alone, as if God had abandoned her. She believed in God's grace, but only for others. Consistent with her desire for perfection, she believed she had to be flawless to gain God's love.

Pointing out the double standard seemed an easy solution, but it was no solution at all. Laura knew she had a double standard. She knew it was not reasonable that God loved others regardless of their behavior, but only loved her based on her performance. She had the head knowledge, but it didn't change the inner conflict. Her efforts continued to be focused on earning God's grace. "I must do better" seemed to be her life motto. Because Laura was engaged in a Jekyll/Hyde battle, dark side versus glossy side, she couldn't see beyond herself and accept the greater truth of grace. But as she moved beyond the Jekyll/Hyde struggle, started looking boldly for truth in her life, and established authentic relationships with others, she began to experience relief from depression and the miracle of grace—from God and others.

Yielding to Hyde. In yielding to Hyde, grace is seen as an opportunity to take advantage of others. It becomes a means of self-fulfillment. Most of us are hesitant to give hitchhikers a ride because of this phenomenon. We've heard stories of drivers offering rides to hitchhikers who have abducted them, stolen their cars, and so on. To the antisocial hitchhiker, the grace of others is an opportunity for personal gain. As with yielding to Jekyll, self is the primary focus and the truth of grace is missed.

Hyde may also see grace as nice, but not much fun compared to tangible pleasures. People often spend their time trying to find happiness in their daily routines and trying to earn enough money to buy more pleasure. One day blends into the next, one paycheck into another. Life slips by, happiness comes and goes, and God watches.

Cheap grace? Evangelicals often talk of "cheap grace." We are told that when we sin, we act as if God's grace was cheap and minimize the suffering of Jesus. This is partly true, but there is more to the story. Sin makes grace abound. We see how vast God's grace really is in response to sin.

Let's say Ron, a devout believer in God, loses his job, his marriage, and his family in a six-month period. He begins struggling with the values he has held for years, and ends up abandoning them and pursuing pleasure. He drinks every night, becomes promiscuous, and experiments with drugs. Several years later his choices bring him to an abrupt dead end when a close friend dies of a drug overdose. He contemplates his situation and returns to God, vowing to live a more consistent, faithful life.

One interpretation is to focus on Ron and discuss how cheap he treated God's grace. God never stopped loving Ron, but Ron turned his back and walked away. This may be true, but the focus is on Ron.

Another interpretation is to focus on God and the incredible nature of God's grace. Nothing Ron did could separate him from God's faithful love or disqualify him from returning to his faith in God. Now the focus is on God.

Sin doesn't make grace cheap, it makes grace abound. Sin brings either self-condemnation (self-focus) or an opportunity to understand the forgiving nature of God who loves regardless of performance (truth-focus).

When I sin, I'm not a victim of cheap grace, but of cheap faith. If I grasp the magnitude of God's grace, then my life will display a strong belief and positive actions. Conversely, if my faith is not big enough to comprehend the "if-less then" of God's grace, my actions will demonstrate self-focused Jekyll/Hyde battles and self-defeating behaviors.

Grace and the Big Picture

Grace is very big—much bigger than a theological concept for Sunday morning sermons. More than any other truth, grace transcends self and separates who we are from what we do. Understanding grace requires us to be truth-focused, because it cannot be understood on a self-focused level. David Seamands, in his book *Healing for Damaged Emotions,* writes:

> We read, we hear, we believe a good theology of grace. But that's not the way we live. We believe grace in our heads but not in our gut level feelings or in our relationships. There's no other word we throw around so piously.

Many speak of grace as if they understand it. But they live differently, investing effort in earning God's favor, condemning themselves when they fail, and focusing on how evil their hidden half is. They talk about grace, but they attempt to understand it with self-focused thinking, which results in guilt because they don't measure up to Jekyll's standards of perfection. Grace must be separated from personal performance in order to be understood.

"Amazing grace! How sweet the sound that saved a wretch like me!" I love the song, but have mixed feelings about the second line. In one sense, I am a wretch. My life (and everyone's life) is marred by sin, by human selfishness, by a desire to usurp control when it is best to submit. But if we spend all our time focusing on human wretchedness, we keep ourselves from looking at God's greatness. God's grace is magnificent whether or not I am a wretch.

A man came up to me after a conference meeting and told me how important it is to understand human evil and our wretched condition (what has been called "worm theology"). He argued that our society has lost sight of the unworthiness of humankind. He was right. We spend so much time trying to convince ourselves that we are okay that we miss the great truth of the spiritual life: We are never okay apart from God. But by focusing so much on human evil, the man missed the greatness of God's grace. It's easy to focus on ourselves—our worthiness or unworthiness—but difficult to get beyond ourselves and focus on someone greater. Grappling with the enormity of grace forces one beyond self.

I found myself observing this man for the remainder of the weekend conference. The following day on the volleyball court, he demonstrated his belief. While the rest of us were having an amusing game of volleyball, he was invested in treating himself harshly. Throughout several games, he muttered about how poorly he was playing and how much better he should be doing. His volleyball philosophy was consistent with his worm theology.

Self-focus leads to shallow spirituality. God doesn't want us to moan in our inadequacies, to be justified by works. God doesn't value us because of our performance. I think God was disappointed that my Christian brother couldn't enjoy his volleyball game, just as God is disappointed when we can't ponder transcendent grace because we are too busy thinking of ourselves as worms.

Wonder theology is an alternative. When Brett first came for counseling, he was overwhelmed by guilt. His sexual behavior had caused many problems and the emotional consequences were catching up with him. During our first session he seemed compelled to confess his awfulness and grovel in his worthlessness. I listened, but didn't actively agree that he was awful. In fact, we didn't talk about his behavior at all. He already knew his behavior was wrong. Instead, we started considering some bigger questions. "What does grace mean?" "How could God still accept Brett?" Without settling for simple answers, we began to explore the profound wonder of God's grace.

Brett did better than most. He modified his worm theology and began contemplating the wonder of God within a few weeks. His symptoms improved, his behaviors changed, and his understanding of God matured. Brett's pain opened his spiritual eyes to a bigger picture of God's grace.

In many ways I am like a worm. When I compare myself to a Creator with such awesome power, I'm pretty small. I'm worthless. In other ways, I'm important. I'm created in God's image. It's quite a paradox—worthless and worthwhile at the same time. It doesn't matter that much. It's more significant that God's love doesn't depend on my value.

Responding to Failure

We are people in conflict, trying to balance desires from the glossy side and dark side while looking for glimpses of truth. Because we struggle, we inevitably fail. Responding to failure becomes important in avoiding future battles of Jekyll and Hyde.

Bonnie had an eating disorder. Each time she binged, she convinced herself it would never happen again. "This time," she reasoned, "I have enough willpower to keep this from happening again." Of course these thoughts were glossy side urges demanding perfection, eventually giving way to dark side urges when she binged again. As Bonnie progressed in treatment, she started responding differently to failure.

Through counseling Bonnie realized she would fail again. She binged about once every two months after treatment; a good improvement from the once-a-day pattern she had when she first sought help. We will always fail again unless we die first. Despite the urgings of the glossy side, we will never be perfect as humans.

Bonnie also learned that failure didn't reduce her worth. Her value no longer depended on her performance. She learned about grace. God's grace and our performance are unrelated. Grace is unconditional.

Glossy side urges controlled Bonnie less after treatment. She still had a "little voice" telling her to eat only celery and to exercise an hour each day, but she filtered that voice through a truth-focused awareness of God. Before treatment she wouldn't eat bread, fearful it would cause her to binge. Now she allowed herself to eat bread and other formerly "forbidden" foods. She became a whole person, in touch with her desires for approval and pleasure and her ability to move beyond both and pursue truth.

How we handle one another's failures is just as important as how we handle our own. With Lisa's help, my children compiled some perspectives on life when they were younger. I especially liked their account entitled "Pretending House."

> You need two people and a baby. The baby could be a doll, a teddy bear, or your little sister. Someone's always the mom (whoever is a girl and pretty big). Someone's always the dad (whoever is a boy and pretty big). If you don't have a boy the biggest girl is the dad. Then we put the baby to bed (you have to pray with her first) and have some pretend tea, or toast, taco or peanut butter sandwiches. When the baby does something like dig in the pretend plants you spank her. Then we talk to her and hug her. Playing pretend house is sort of like real life even.

Though we tried to use spanking rarely in our discipline, I like the way my children described their spankings. Spankings were followed with affirmation. Children are worthwhile, even when they have transgressed. Expressing their worth is an integral part of good discipline. I want my children to experience grace in the way I treat them, so they can understand a purer form of grace in God.

Grace Works Better than Jekyll or Hyde

The Jekyll/Hyde struggle is uncomfortable, so we try to escape it. But our efforts to destroy dark side urges result in stronger glossy side urges as the Jekyll/Hyde battle escalates and self-focus becomes a way of life. In the midst of the battle we can't see grace. The bigger picture gets fuzzy as the "shoulds" of Jekyll battle the "wants" of Hyde.

Quick-fixes relieve the battle for a while but keep the focus on self, causing missed opportunities for growth, shallow spirituality, and lack of insight. Trying to eliminate, rather than manage, Jekyll and Hyde keeps us from understanding God's grace.

What Do We Need?

What do we need most in society today? We need whole persons who understand grace. We certainly don't need more newspaper scandals or more sexual game-playing. We don't need bigger ministries, more popular television evangelists, or Christian amusement parks. We don't need more eloquent pastors or persuasive authors or cogent speakers. We don't need bigger organizations or larger budgets. We don't even need more psychologists or more seminaries. We simply need sincerity. We need people who understand grace and live authentically. We need whole persons.

Grace allows wholeness. Because God accepts us and loves us despite our struggles with Jekyll and Hyde, we can be whole before God, assured of love. Recognizing our completeness in God allows us to rest in the deep joy of true spirituality. It allows us to take our eyes off ourselves and gaze intently at God.

We experience wholeness as we move beyond the Jekyll/Hyde battles. Engaged in a compelling search for truth, we articulate values and a mission in life, relate authentically with others, and look beyond ourselves. God's grace begins to absorb self-interest and urges for pleasure and approval become stepping stones to greater understanding and wholeness.

CONCLUSION

PRACTICE MAKES BETTER

Several of my family members, including me, are trying to learn to juggle. The difficult part for us, as novices, is managing three balls with two hands. As a child I used to say I could juggle two balls. But that's not really juggling. Now that I'm trying to juggle the right way, I'm filled with questions. When do I let go of this one? How do I catch that one when I've just finished letting go of another? What do I do with the one that's in the air? with my right hand? with my left hand?

Those who have juggled for some time make it look easy. They have trained themselves to do it efficiently. The juggling experts' brains probably look like rural highways—working smoothly with minimal activity. If we could observe my brain activity while juggling, I suspect we would see millions of neurons firing like a Boston traffic jam.

A similar principle can be seen in driving. The sixteen year-old taking a driving test is overwhelmed with inefficient brain activity, and still may not be a great driver. But ten years later the same person is driving down the freeway at 65 mph, eating a Whopper, and talking on the cellular phone at the same time. Driving, like juggling, requires less concentration as experience is gained.

Learning authenticity is a bit like juggling. It feels natural to those who have done it for a long time. For those just learning, it feels like a lot to learn. We're trying to keep track of our desire for pleasure (Hyde), our desire for approval (Jekyll), while still leaving time for the truth-focused part of personality. If we spend too much or too little time holding one of the balls, some of the balls get dropped.

Becoming authentic in our superficial culture is a bit like juggling in a windstorm. All around us are pressures to remain hidden and self-protective, to pretend we are invulnerable and invincible, to look as good as fashion models, to smile as much as politicians, to know as much as Jeopardy contestants. It's hard to be authentic in the midst of such a culture.

Sometimes people overcompensate in a windstorm like this. Instead of conforming to demands to be perfect, some decide to be absolutely authentic—to air every feeling, to discuss every disgusting thought, to speak every unspeakable fantasy. Soon the scars of rejection and pain of embarrassment drive them back into hiding.

Somewhere between the two extremes is a balance point where we shed the unrealistic expectations of our culture, yet find safe places to be vulnerable and honest. Striking the balance takes practice—like juggling in the wind. If we expect ourselves to suddenly get it right, to be completely authentic, entirely wise, totally humble, we expect too much. The task of authentic living is too big to master with one book or one resolution. It takes practice. But each time we tell ourselves and an intimate friend the truth, we move one step deeper into a life of authenticity.